ANTI-INFLAMMATORY DIE COOKBOOK FOR BEGINNERS 2022

1200 DAYS OF EASY & TASTY HEALTHY RECIPES WITH A 30 DAYS MEAL PLAN TO REDUCE INFLAMMATION AND BALANCE HORMONES

Poula Ray

1

Table of Contents

1.   Introduction

As we know, inflammation is actually one of the major causes of many other diseases. Inflammation is a natural process of our body response system if any foreign invaders such as bacteria or viruses enter our body. In this situation, our immune system comes into action and attacks it. This is also called an immune response, but sometimes it goes wrong. Our immune system mistakenly recognizes healthy cells and tissues are harmful. This may cause inflammation. It is linked with various diseases like Alzheimer's, arthritis, heart disease, type-2 diabetes, cancer, and many other diseases. There are various ways to treat inflammation, such as supplements, steroids, non-steroidal anti-inflammatory drugs. The most natural way to fight against inflammation is to adopt an anti-inflammatory food-eating lifestyle.

Several factors cause inflammation, but one of the major causes of the inflammation is following a poor diet. Eating unhealthy food can trigger inflammation in our bodies. A poor diet is linked with various inflammatory diseases. Therefore, it is important to improve our daily diet to naturally trigger our body's anti-inflammatory response. Many people suffer due to chronic or acute inflammation. Adopting an anti-inflammatory diet helps with your medical conditions and makes you physically and mentally strong. This cookbook will help you to know about an anti-inflammatory diet.

Chapter 1:   Anti-Inflammatory Diet's Main Advantages

According to research, eating an anti-inflammatory diet may help relieve the symptoms of various diseases.

The formation of plaque in the arteries is known as atherosclerosis, and it is quite prevalent among the elderly. The researchers discovered a correlation between subclinical atherosclerosis and heart disease-related mortality; following an anti-inflammatory diet may assist people with type 2 diabetes decrease certain inflammatory markers. Individuals with type 2 diabetes who follow the Mediterranean diet solely report fewer inflammation symptoms than those who do not follow an anti-inflammatory diet.

The Mediterranean diet and the anti-inflammatory diet have a lot in common. The Mediterranean diet emphasizes low-fat dairy products and the selection and preparation of protein-rich meals. Mediterranean diet followers favor plant-based proteins such as beans, nuts, and seeds, which may also offer enough dietary fiber. As previously stated, antioxidants are necessary for our diets to help prevent or postpone cell damage. You should choose vegetables and fruits of various colors to help manage inflammation and deliver consistent energy. Minerals and vitamins, vital fatty acids, dietary fiber, and beneficial phytonutrients should all be included in an anti-inflammatory diet.

Furthermore, following an anti-inflammatory diet might assist you in preventing becoming obese. An anti-inflammatory diet warns against eating too many calories, leading to fat tissue buildup and obesity.

Obesity and an inflammatory diet may be linked in numerous ways. One inflammatory diet is consuming more refined carbs, processed meats, and junk food. Because of the low-calorie content and lack of fiber in these meals, a person will have to compensate for the calorie deficit and lack of satiety by eating more. Two, someone who eats an inflammatory diet may spend more time sitting inside, thereby encouraging them to consume more calories and move less.

An anti-inflammatory diet, in particular, may aid people who are already suffering from inflammatory disorders. Anti-inflammatory diets that exclude refined sugars and carbohydrates, for example, may lead to type 2 diabetes, metabolic syndrome, and obesity. Instead, an anti-inflammatory diet recommends eating whole grains like brown rice, which is high in fiber and low glycemic index.

In this way, following an anti-inflammatory diet improves one's long-term health. In an anti-inflammatory diet, saturated and trans-fatty acids are avoided in omega-3 fatty acids. Unhealthy fat consumption has been linked to an increased risk of cardiovascular disease. One of the negative consequences of bad fats is that they deposit on the inside walls of blood vessels, narrowing them and raising blood pressure. Increased blood pressure may harm blood vessels and other organs that respond to a higher than normal blood flow rate. The anti-inflammatory diet encourages heart-healthy oils like olive oil and flaxseed.

With this in actual mind, an anti-inflammatory diet is essential for long-term blood pressure management.

An anti-inflammatory diet may also help with weariness. The inflammation indicates that the immune system is working. Histamine levels rise when the immune system gets completely dedicated, making a person feel sleepy, tired, and cranky. The immune system's operations are supposed to cause weariness, which allows your body to slow down and preserve energy. Fatigue is also thought to aid rest and healing rather than further limiting the body. An anti-inflammatory diet helps to reduce or eliminate inflammation, which reduces or eliminates the immune system's fatigue-causing effects.

An anti-inflammatory diet, which has nothing to do with obesity, may help you lose weight. You might be overweight or on the verge of being obese even if you are not obese. Unintentional weight gain and other non-dietary reasons, such as sedentary lifestyles, blame on the high consumption of refined carbs and sugars. Refined carbohydrate foods are deficient in nutrients, meaning that one must eat more calories than required to meet calorie requirements. Furthermore, refined carbohydrate foods lack fiber, causing people to overeat about their physical size since they don't feel full. Fortunately, an anti-inflammatory diet excludes refined carbs and promotes other nutrient-dense foods, meaning that harmful sugars and carbohydrates are avoided.

Following an anti-inflammatory diet also has indirect advantages.

One of these advantages is that a person will feel more settled due to dietary choices that reduce inflammation. Pain, weariness, swelling, and immobility are some of the symptoms of inflammation.

Inflammation, in this context, may lead to absence from work or school. Inflammation may cause pain at work or school, making it difficult to concentrate. An individual's chances of achieving desired attention at work or school will improve if dietary sources of inflammation are addressed.

An anti-inflammatory diet may help you sleep better. In various ways, diet may contribute to poor sleep quality or an inconsistent sleep pattern. When you eat a diet that raises inflammation, you'll have trouble sleeping regularly, and when you do, it'll be of poor quality. An inflammatory diet may lead to eating problems, such as getting up in the middle of the night to eat, disrupting the quality and length of sleep. You may need frequent episodes of brief sleeping due to weariness, which will disrupt your night's sleep. Fortunately, an anti-inflammatory diet may help you sleep better by reducing inflammation and ensuring that your meals are balanced in terms of calories and minerals.

Finally, an anti-inflammatory diet encourages diversity and choice, enabling other dietary regimens to draw inspiration. An anti-inflammatory diet refers to reducing or eliminating inflammation while still providing the nutrients and calories required for daily consumption. Several diets, such as vegan and Mediterranean diets, match the anti-inflammatory diet. An anti-inflammatory diet enables people to make their own choices, which is a key aspect of the success of any dietary strategy. Because of availability, cost, cultural relevance, and seasonality, openness in a dietary plan are required.

Chapter 2:   Diet Tips to Help You Fight Inflammation

Choosing entire meals like fruits, vegetables & whole grains over processed meals has several health advantages. One of the most important advantages of these nutrient-dense meals is their ability to decrease inflammation in the body.

Dietary Recommendations for Food

Patton offers nine dietary guidelines for reducing inflammation:

- Whole-grain carbohydrates, pure whole fruits and veggies are the best options.

- To get the most nutritious bang for your money, rotate among a range of colorful fruits, veggies, and grains from week to week.

- Refined starches (white variants) and added sugars should be avoided (brown or white sugar, energy drinks, soda). Inflammatory symptoms, including weight gain and increased blood glucose and cholesterol levels, are promoted by these less nutrient-dense diets.

- Processed meats like salami, bologna and hot dogs, as well as high-fat red meats like prime rib, bacon, and sausage, should be avoided. These are high in saturated fat, which may cause inflammation if ingested in excess.

- Omega-3 and Monounsaturated fats are recommended because they are thought to reduce inflammation. Olive oil, avocados, and almonds all contain monounsaturated fats. Consumption of these fats has been linked to a lower risk of cancer and heart disease, both of which are linked to inflammation.

- Tuna and wild salmon, walnuts, and ground flaxseed all contain omega-3 fatty acids. Omega-3 is an important fatty acid that our systems cannot produce and must be obtained via food or supplementation.

- Saturated fat should be avoided. Whole milk, cheese, butter, high-fat red meat, and chicken skin all fall under this category. Because our bodies only need a tiny quantity, every day over consumption will increase the inflammatory response.

- Trans fat should be avoided if possible. While trans fats have been prohibited in most foods by the FDA, they may still be found in products like flavored coffee creamers and microwave popcorn. As a result, make sure to read labels carefully. There is no such thing as a safe level of trans fat. It not only lowers good cholesterol while raising bad cholesterol (a pro-inflammatory factor), but it also reuses and recycles it.

Find Vitamins in foods you consume

Here are some suggestions that are most effective for people who exercise frequently:

- Vitamin A: is found in sweet potatoes, spinach, carrots, and tomatoes, among other foods.

- Vitamin C: is present in fruits and vegetables such as citrus, cantaloupe, and green & red peppers.

- Vitamin D: Oily fish, fortified meals, and dairy products are all good sources of vitamin D.

- Calcium: Cheese, low-fat milk, kale, broccoli, fortified orange juice, low-fat Greek yogurt, and fortified non-dairy milk are all good sources of calcium.

- Copper: To obtain your copper, eat pumpkin, sesame, shitake mushrooms, sunflower seeds and pumpkin, and cashews. Copper is also beneficial during the first several weeks after an injury (a sufficient quantity can be found in a normal multivitamin).

- Zinc: Eat crabmeat, chicken, lean beef, cashews, and fortified cereals to increase your zinc intake.

- Turmeric: Turmeric is a spice that may be found in curry powder. Curcumin is an anti-inflammatory, antioxidant chemical found in turmeric, which provides mustard and curries their yellow color. Probably add turmeric to your spice cabinet, or take 400 milligrams of turmeric daily in pill form for a more aggressive approach.

- Garlic: It may help maintain arteries flexible and clean, enabling oxygen-rich blood to reach working muscles by reducing the production of 2 inflammatory enzymes. Cooking with 2 to 4 garlic cloves each day will enhance taste and help to reduce inflammation.

- Bromelain: Bromelain is a pineapple-derived enzyme. After your exercise, drink one glass of pineapple juice or include it in your recovery smoothie for lots of immune-boosting vitamin C & inflammation-fighting effects.

"It's important to think about how you nourish your body," she advises. "A healthy diet and vitamins may help keep inflammation under control."

Chapter 3:   Breakfast Recipes

Recipe 1:   Baked Eggs with Portobello Mushrooms

Serving Size: 4

Cooking Time: 20 minutes

Ingredients:

- 4 Portobello mushroom caps
- 1 cup arugula
- 1 medium tomato, chopped
- 4 large eggs, pasture-raised
- Salt and pepper to taste

Directions:

1. Preheat the oven to a heat of 350°F and line a baking sheet with parchment paper.
2. Scoop out the gills from the mushrooms using a spoon. Discard the gills and set them aside.
3. Place the mushrooms on the baking sheet inverted (gill side up) and fill each cap with arugula and tomato.
4. Carefully crack an egg on each mushroom cap.
5. Bake in the oven for 20 minutes or until the eggs have been set.

Nutritional Value: Calories 180; Fat 10g; Carbohydrates 5g; Protein 5g

Recipe 2: Beef Breakfast Casserole

Serving Size: 5

Cooking Time: 30 minutes

Ingredients:

- 1 lb ground beef, cooked
- 10 eggs
- ½ cup Pico de Gallo
- 1 cup baby spinach
- ¼ cup sliced black olives
- Freshly ground black pepper

Directions:

1. Preheat the oven to 350°F. Prepare a 9" glass pie plate with non-stick spray.
2. Whisk the eggs until frothy. Season with salt and pepper.
3. Layer the cooked ground beef, Pico de Gallo, and spinach on the pie plate.
4. Slowly pour the eggs over the top.
5. Top with black olives.
6. Bake for at least 30 minutes until firm in the middle.
7. Slice into 5 pieces and serve.

Nutritional Value: Calories 479; Fat 30.5g; Carbohydrates 4.65g; Protein 43.5g

Recipe 3: Blueberry Sweet Potato Breakfast Meatballs

Serving Size: 8

Cooking Time: 20 minutes

Ingredients:

- 1 large sweet potato, peeled
- 2 lb ground pork (may also use turkey)
- 1 1/2 cups kale, chopped and de-stemmed
- 2/3 cup blueberries
- 1 tablespoon pure maple syrup
- 1 1/2 teaspoon coarse sea salt
- 1 1/2 teaspoon fresh chopped thyme (may substitute 3/4 teaspoon dried)
- 1 1/2 teaspoon fresh chopped sage (may substitute 3/4 teaspoon dried)

Directions:

1. Preheat the oven to 400°F and dress a baking tray with parchment paper.
2. Grate the sweet potato until you have 1 1/2 cups. Place it in a mixing bowl with the pork, kale, blueberries, syrup, salt, thyme, and sage. Stir gently to make sure it is well combined. You may have to use your hands; try not to crush the blueberries.
3. Form the mixture into balls then place them on the prepared baking tray.
4. Bake for 20 minutes, or until the meatballs are nicely browned.

Nutritional Value: Calories 374; Fat 24g; Carbohydrates 9g; Protein 30g

Recipe 4: Blueberry-Topped Steel-Cut Oats

Serving Size: 4

Cooking Time: 10 minutes

Ingredients:

- 2 cups steel-cut oats
- 3 cups water
- 1/2 teaspoon ground cinnamon
- Pinch sea salt
- 1/4 cup maple syrup
- 1/2 to 1 cup non dairy milk
- 1 cup of fresh blueberries, for serving

Directions:

1. In the Instant Pot, combine the oats, water, cinnamon, and salt. Lock the lid.
2. Select Pressure Cook, then cook at high pressure for 10 minutes.
3. When cooking is complete, use a natural release.
4. Remove the lid, then stir in the maple syrup and as much milk as you need to get the consistency you prefer (more milk makes the oats creamier).
5. Top each serving with 1/4 cup of blueberries to serve.

Nutritional Value: Calories 382; Fat 5.5g; Carbohydrates 3g; Protein 10g

Recipe 5:   Breakfast Spinach Mushroom Tomato Fry Up

Serving Size: 2

Cooking Time: 10 minutes

Ingredients:

- 1 teaspoon olive oil
- 1 red onion, sliced
- 6 button mushrooms, sliced
- ½ cup cherry tomatoes, halved
- ½ teaspoon diced lemon rind
- 3 large handfuls baby spinach
- Salt and pepper to taste

Directions:

1. Heat oil in a skillet over medium-low heat.
2. Sauté the onion until fragrant.
3. Add in the mushrooms and tomatoes. Season with lemon rind, salt and pepper. Cook for another 5 minutes.
4. Stir in the baby spinach until wilted.

Nutritional Value: Calories 83; Fat 3g; Carbohydrates 3g; Protein 2g

Recipe 6: Buckwheat and Chia Seed Overnight Oats

Serving Size: 4

Cooking Time: 10 minutes

Ingredients:

- 1 cup gluten-free rolled oats
- 1/4 cup buckwheat groats
- 2 tablespoon chopped almonds
- 3 tablespoon chia seeds
- 1 cups blueberries (fresh or frozen)
- 1 clementine orange, peeled
- 2 cups unsweetened almond milk
- 2 dates, pitted
- 1 tablespoon ground flaxseed
- 1/4 teaspoon ground ginger
- Optional toppings: blueberries, banana slices, raspberries, chia seeds, walnuts, chopped dates

Directions:

1. In a huge bowl, combine the oats, buckwheat groats, almonds, and chia seeds, and stir to combine.
2. In a blender, purée the blueberries, orange, almond milk, dates, flax, and ginger. The mixture should have a smooth consistency.
3. Stir the blended mixture into the oat mixture until well combined.
4. Cover the bowl with plastic wrap and refrigerate overnight.
5. Serve in the morning with whatever toppings you like.

Nutritional Value: Calories 272; Fat 8g; Carbohydrates 46g; Protein 9g

Recipe 7: Coconut Porridge with Strawberries

Serving Size: 2

Cooking Time: 15 minutes

Ingredients:

- 1 egg
- 2 teaspoon olive oil
- 1 tablespoon coconut flour
- 1 pinch ground chia seeds
- 5 tablespoon coconut cream
- Thawed frozen strawberries

Directions:

1. Place a large-sized nonstick saucepan over low heat and pour in the olive oil, egg, coconut flour, chia seeds, and coconut cream.
2. Cook the mixture while stirring continuously until your desired consistency is achieved.
3. Turn the heat off and spoon the porridge into serving bowls.
4. Top with 4 to 6 strawberries and serve immediately.

Nutritional Value: Calories 210; Fat 27g; Carbohydrates 20g; Protein 9g

Recipe 8: Crispy Chicken Fingers

Serving Size: 6

Cooking Time: 20 minutes

Ingredients:

- ⅔ cup almond meal
- Salt and black pepper
- ½ teaspoon ground turmeric
- ½ teaspoon red pepper cayenne
- ½ teaspoon garlic powder
- 1 egg
- 1 lb chicken breasts, cut into strips
- ½ teaspoon paprika

Directions:

1. Preheat the oven to 375°F. Line a substantial baking sheet with parchment paper.
2. In a shallow dish, beat the egg.
3. In another shallow dish, mix almond meal and spices.
4. Coat each chicken strip with egg after which roll into the spice mixture evenly.
5. Arrange the chicken strips onto the prepared baking sheet in a single layer.
6. Bake for approximately 16 to 18 minutes.

Nutritional Value: Calories 236; Fat 10g; Carbohydrates 26g; Protein 37g

Recipe 9: Dijon-Style Deviled Eggs

Serving Size: 6

Cooking Time: 20 minutes

Ingredients:

- 6 eggs
- 1 cup cream cheese, softened
- 1 teaspoon Dijon mustard
- ¼ teaspoon turmeric powder
- Salt and pepper to taste
- 4 oz smoked salmon, sliced
- 1 tablespoon chopped fresh dill

Directions:

1. Place the eggs in boiling salted water in a pot over medium heat and cook them for 10 minutes. Transfer to an ice-water bath. Let cool for 5 minutes, peel, and slice in half. Remove the yolks to a bowl and put the whites on a plate.
2. Mash the yolks with a fork and add the cream cheese, Dijon mustard, salt, pepper, and turmeric. Spoon the prepared mixture into a piping bag and fill into the egg whites. Top with smoked salmon and dill and serve.

Nutritional Value: Calories 317; Fat 10g; Carbohydrates 50.6g; Protein 7g

Recipe 10: Ham and Veggie Frittata Muffins

Serving Size: 12

Cooking Time: 25 minutes

Ingredients:

- 5 oz thinly sliced ham
- 8 large eggs
- 4 tablespoon coconut oil
- ½ yellow onion, finely diced
- 8 oz frozen spinach, thawed and drained
- 8 oz mushrooms, thinly sliced
- 1 cup cherry tomatoes, halved
- ¼ cup coconut milk (canned)
- 2 tablespoon coconut flour
- Sea salt and pepper to taste

Directions:

1. Preheat the oven to 375°F.
2. In a medium skillet, warm the coconut oil on medium heat. Add the onion and cook until softened.
3. Add the mushrooms, spinach, and cherry tomatoes. Season with salt and pepper. Cook until the mushrooms have softened. About 5 minutes. Remove from heat and set aside.
4. In a huge bowl, beat the eggs together with coconut milk and coconut flour. Stir in the cooled veggie mixture.
5. Line each cavity of a 12 cavity muffin tin with the thinly sliced ham. Pour the egg mixture into each one and bake for 20 minutes.
6. Remove from oven and allow to cool for about 5 minutes before transferring to a wire rack.
7. To maximize the benefit of a vegetable-rich diet, it's important to eat a variety of colors, and these veggie-packed frittata muffins do just that. The onion, spinach, mushrooms, and cherry tomatoes provide a wide range of vitamins and nutrients and a healthy dose of fiber.

Nutritional Value: Calories 125; Fat 9.8g; Carbohydrates 4.4g; Protein 5.9g

Recipe 11: Hash Browns

Serving Size: 4

Cooking Time: 15 minutes

Ingredients:

- 1-pound Russet potatoes, peeled, processed using a grater
- Pinch of sea salt
- Pinch of black pepper to taste
- 3 tablespoons olive oil

Directions:

1. Paper towels should actually be used to line a microwave-safe dish. On top, strew shredded potatoes. Microwave the vegetables for 2 minutes on high heat. Remove the pan from the heat.
2. In a large-sized nonstick skillet over medium heat, pour 1 tablespoon of oil.
3. Place a large pinch of potatoes into the heated oil in batches. Using the back of a prepared spatula, press down.
4. Cook for 3 minutes on each side, or until crispy and golden. Using paper towels, absorb any excess liquid. Carry on with the rest of the potatoes in the same manner. As required, add extra oil.
5. Salt & pepper to taste. Serve.

Nutritional Value: Calories 200; Fat 11.7g; Carbohydrates 20.4g; Protein 4.3g

Recipe 12: Lemon-Almond Waffles

Serving Size: 4

Cooking Time: 20 minutes

Ingredients:

- 3 eggs
- 2/3 cup almond flour
- 2 ½ teaspoon baking powder
- A pinch of sea salt
- 1 ½ cups almond milk
- 2 tablespoon olive oil
- 1 cup fresh almond butter
- 2 tablespoon pure maple syrup
- 1 teaspoon fresh lemon juice

Directions:

1. Place the eggs, almond flour, baking powder, salt, and almond milk in a medium bowl. Mix until well combined. Preheat a waffle iron and brush with a bit of olive oil. Pour in a quarter cup of the batter, close the iron and cook until the waffles are golden and crisp, 2-3 minutes.
2. Transfer the waffles to a plate and make more waffles until the ingredients are exhausted. Mix the prepared almond butter with maple syrup and lemon juice in a bowl. Spread the top with the almond-lemon mixture and serve.

Nutritional Value: Calories 430; Fat 40g; Carbohydrates 16.7g; Protein 7g

Recipe 13: Millet-Blueberry Bake with Applesauce

Serving Size: 8

Cooking Time: 55 minutes

Ingredients:

- 2 cups millet, soaked in water overnight
- 2 cups fresh or frozen blueberries
- 1¾ cups unsweetened applesauce
- ⅓ cup coconut oil, melted
- 2 teaspoons grated fresh ginger
- 1½ teaspoons ground cinnamon

Directions:

1. In a fine-mesh sieve, drain and rinse the millet for 1 to 2 minutes. Transfer to a large bowl.
2. Gently fold in the blueberries, applesauce, coconut oil, ginger, and cinnamon.
3. Pour the prepared mixture into a 9-by-9-inch casserole dish. Cover with aluminum foil.
4. Place the dish in the preheated oven and bake for 40 minutes. Remove the foil and bake for 10 to 15 minutes more, or until lightly crisp on top.

Nutritional Value: Calories 323; Fat 13g; Carbohydrates 48g; Protein 6g

Recipe 14: Oatmeal Pancakes

Serving Size: 2

Cooking Time: 10 minutes

Ingredients:

- 1 ½ cup rolled oats, whole-grain
- 2 eggs, large & pastured
- 2 teaspoon Baking Powder
- 1 banana, ripe
- 2 tablespoon water
- ¼ cup maple syrup
- 1 teaspoon vanilla extract
- 2 tablespoon extra virgin olive oil

Directions:

1. To make this delicious breakfast dish, you need to first blend all the ingredients in a high-speed blender for a minute or two or until you get a smooth batter. Tip: To blend easily, pour egg, banana, and all other liquid ingredients first and finally add oats at the end.
2. Now, take a large-sized skillet and heat it over medium-low heat.
3. Once the skillet is hot, ¼ cup of the batter into it and cook it for 3 to 4 minutes per side or until bubbles start appearing in the middle portion.
4. Turn the pancake and cook the other side also.
5. Serve warm.

Nutritional Value: Calories 201; Fat 7g; Carbohydrates 27g; Protein 5g

Recipe 15: Oregano Scramble with Cherry Tomatoes

Serving Size: 2

Cooking Time: 10 minutes

Ingredients:

- 4 eggs
- 2 teaspoons chopped fresh oregano
- 1 tablespoon extra-virgin olive oil
- 1 cup halved cherry tomatoes
- ½ garlic clove, sliced
- ½ avocado, sliced

Directions:

1. In a large-sized bowl, beat the eggs until well combined; whisk in the oregano.
2. Place a large skillet over medium heat. Once the large-sized pan is hot, add the olive oil.
3. Pour the eggs into the skillet and use either a heat-resistant spatula or wooden spoon to scramble the eggs. Transfer the eggs to a serving dish.
4. Add the cherry tomatoes and garlic to the pan and sauté for about 2 minutes. Spoon the tomatoes over the eggs and top the dish with the avocado slices.

Nutritional Value: Calories 310; Fat 26g; Carbohydrates 10g; Protein 13g

Recipe 16: Quinoa and Cauliflower Congee

Serving Size: 8

Cooking Time: 1 hour

Ingredients:

- 1 cauliflower head, minced
- 2 tablespoons red quinoa
- 2 leeks, minced
- 1 tablespoon fresh ginger, grated
- 2 garlic cloves, grated
- 6 cups of water
- 2 tablespoons brown rice
- 1 tablespoon olive oil
- 1 tablespoon fish sauce
- 2 onions, minced
- Pinch of white pepper

For Garnish

- 4 eggs, soft-boiled
- 2 red chili, minced
- 1 lime, sliced into wedges
- ¼ cup packed basil leaves, torn
- ¼ cup loosely packed cilantro leaves, torn
- ¼ cup loosely packed spearmint leaves, torn

Directions:

1. Put olive oil into a huge skillet on medium heat. Sauté shallots, garlic, and ginger until limp and aromatic; pour into a slow cooker set at medium heat.
2. Except for garnishes, pour remaining ingredients into slow cooker; stir. Put the lid on. Cook for 6 hours. Turn off heat. Taste; adjust seasoning if needed.
3. Ladle congee into individual bowls. Garnish with basil leaves, cilantro leaves, red chilli, and spearmint leaves. Add 1 piece of soft-boiled egg on top of each; serve with a wedge of lime on the side. Slice egg just before eating so yolk runs into congee. Squeeze lime juice into congee just before eating.

Nutritional Value: Calories 138; Fat 7.65g; Carbohydrates 10.7g; Protein 7.3g

Recipe 17: Salmon and Egg Scramble

Serving Size: 4

Cooking Time: 15 minutes

Ingredients:

- 6 oz smoked salmon, flaked
- 2 tablespoon extra-virgin olive oil
- 8 eggs, beaten
- ¼ teaspoon ground black pepper

Directions:

1. Warm the prepared olive oil in a large nonstick skillet over medium heat.
2. Add the salmon and cook for 3 minutes, stirring.
3. In a large-sized bowl, whisk the eggs and pepper.
4. Add them to the skillet and cook for about 5 minutes.
5. Serve warm.

Nutritional Value: Calories 235; Fat 19g; Carbohydrates 2g; Protein 19g

Recipe 18: Scotch Eggs with Ground Turkey

Serving Size: 2

Cooking Time: 10 minutes

Ingredients:

- 16 ounces (454 g) lean ground turkey
- ½ teaspoon black pepper
- ½ teaspoon nutmeg
- ½ teaspoon cinnamon
- ½ teaspoon cloves
- ½ teaspoon dried tarragon
- ½ cup finely chopped fresh parsley
- ½ tablespoon dried chives
- 1 clove garlic, finely chopped
- 4 free-range eggs, boiled and peeled

Directions:

1. Preheat the oven to a heat of 375°F (190°C).
2. Cover a baking sheet with parchment paper.
3. Combine the turkey with the cinnamon, nutmeg, pepper, cloves, tarragon, chives, parsley and garlic in a mixing bowl and mix with your hands until thoroughly mixed.
4. Divide the mixture into 4 circular shapes with the palms of your hands.
5. Flatten each one into a pancake shape using the backs of your hands or a rolling pin.
6. Wrap the meat pancake around 1 egg, until it's covered. (You can moisten the meat with water first to help prevent it from sticking to your hands).
7. Bake in the oven for approximately about 25 minutes or until brown and crisp. Serve.

Nutritional Value: Calories 502; Fat 30g; Carbohydrates 55g; Protein 3g

Recipe 19: Scrambled Eggs with Smoked Salmon

Serving Size: 4

Cooking Time: 15 minutes

Ingredients:

- 2 chopped chives, chopped
- 2 tablespoon olive oil
- 6 oz smoked salmon, flaked
- 8 eggs, beaten
- ¼ teaspoon ground black pepper

Directions:

1. Warm the olive oil in a large-sized skillet over medium heat and cook the salmon for 3 minutes, stirring often.
2. Beat the eggs and pepper in a bowl, pour it over the salmon, and cook for 5 minutes, stirring gently until set.
3. Top with chives and serve warm.

Nutritional Value: Calories 240; Fat 19g; Carbohydrates 1g; Protein 17g

Recipe 20: Scrambled Tofu with Bell Pepper

Serving Size: 4

Cooking Time: 20 minutes

Ingredients:

- 2 tablespoon olive oil
- 1 (14-oz) firm tofu, crumbled
- 1 red bell pepper, chopped
- 1 green bell pepper, chopped
- 1 tomato, finely chopped
- 2 chopped green onions
- Sea salt and pepper to taste
- 1 teaspoon turmeric powder
- 1 teaspoon Creole seasoning
- ½ cup chopped baby kale
- ¼ cup grated Parmesan

Directions:

1. Warm the olive oil in a large-sized skillet over medium heat and add the tofu. Cook with occasional stirring until the tofu is light golden brown while making sure not to break the tofu into tiny bits but to have scrambled egg resemblance, 5 minutes.
2. Stir in the bell peppers, tomato, green onions, salt, pepper, turmeric powder, and Creole seasoning. Sauté until the vegetables soften, 5 minutes. Stir in the kale for 3 minutes until wilts. Add half of the Parmesan cheese and stir for 1-2 minutes until melted.
3. Turn the heat off. Top with the remaining cheese and serve.

Nutritional Value: Calories 159; Fat 11g; Carbohydrates 7.1g; Protein 10g

Recipe 21: Spicy Marble Eggs

Serving Size: 12

Cooking Time: 15 minutes

Ingredients:

- 6 medium-boiled eggs, unpeeled, cooled

For the Marinade:

- 2 oolong black tea bags
- 3 tablespoon brown sugar
- 1 thumb-sized fresh ginger, unpeeled, crushed
- 3 dried star anise, whole
- 2 dried bay leaves
- 3 tablespoon light soy sauce
- 4 tablespoon dark soy sauce
- 4 cups water
- 1 dried cinnamon stick, whole
- 1 teaspoon salt
- 1 teaspoon dried Szechuan peppercorns

Directions:

1. Using the back of a metal spoon, crack eggshells in places to create a spider web effect. Do not peel. Set aside until needed. Pour marinade into a large Dutch oven set over high heat. Put lid partially on. Bring water to a rolling boil for about 5 minutes. Turn off the heat. Secure lid. Steep ingredients for 10 minutes.
2. Using a slotted spoon, fish out and discard solids. Cool marinade completely to the room proceeding. Place eggs into an airtight non-reactive container just small enough to snugly fit all this in.
3. Pour in marinade. Eggs should be completely submerged in liquid. Discard leftover marinade, if any. Line container rim with generous layers of saran wrap. Secure container lid.
4. Chill eggs for 24 hours before using. Extract eggs and drain each piece well before using, but keep the rest submerged in the marinade.

Nutritional Value: Calories 75; Fat 4.3g; Carbohydrates 4.8g; Protein 4.05g

Recipe 22: Spicy Quinoa

Serving Size: 2

Cooking Time: 20 minutes

Ingredients:

- 1 cup water
- ¼ cup hemp seeds
- ½ teaspoon ground cinnamon
- Pinch salt
- ¼ cup chopped hazelnuts
- ½ cup quinoa rinsed well
- ¼ cup shredded coconut
- 1 tablespoon flaxseed
- ½ teaspoon vanilla extract
- ½ cup fresh berries of your choice, divided

Directions:

1. Combine the prepared quinoa and water in a medium saucepan over high heat.
2. Set to a boil, then lower to low heat and continue to cook for 15 to 20 minutes until the quinoa is tender.
3. Combine coconut, flaxseed, hemp seeds, cinnamon, vanilla, and salt in a large mixing bowl.
4. Divide the quinoa into 2 bowls and finish with some berries and hazelnuts for each serving.

Nutritional Value: Calories 286; Fat 13g; Carbohydrates 32g; Protein 10g

Recipe 23: Spinach Breakfast

Serving Size: 4

Cooking Time: 35 minutes

Ingredients:

- 2 sweet potatoes, peeled and diced
- 2 tablespoon olive oil
- ½ teaspoon onion powder
- ½ teaspoon garlic powder
- ¼ teaspoon paprika
- 4 eggs, pasture-raised
- ½ onion, sliced
- ½ cup mushrooms, sliced
- 2 cups fresh baby spinach
- Salt and pepper to taste
- Coconut oil for greasing

Directions:

1. Preheat the oven to 425°F.
2. Place the prepared potatoes in a baking dish and drizzle with olive oil. Season with onion powder, garlic powder, paprika, salt, and pepper to taste. Once cooked, set aside.
3. Bake in the oven for 30 minutes while turning the sweet potatoes halfway through the cooking time.
4. Heat skillet and grease with coconut oil.
5. Sauté the onion for 30 seconds until fragrant.
6. Add in the mushrooms and egg. Season with salt and pepper to taste.
7. Scramble the eggs.
8. Before the eggs have set, stir in the baby spinach until wilted.
9. Plate the potatoes and top with the egg mixture.

Nutritional Value: Calories 252; Fat 17g; Carbohydrates 15g; Protein 11g

Recipe 24: Sweet Potato and Cauliflower Hash Browns

Serving Size: 4

Cooking Time: 35 minutes

Ingredients:

- 3 eggs
- 2 sweet potatoes, shredded
- 1 big head cauliflower, riced
- ½ white onion, grated
- Sea salt and pepper to taste
- 4 tablespoon olive oil

Directions:

1. In a bowl, mix the eggs, sweet potatoes, cauliflower, onion, salt, and black pepper until well combined. Allow sitting for 5 minutes to thicken. Working in batches, brush a nonstick skillet with olive oil and add 4 scoops of the hash brown mixture to the skillet.
2. Make sure to have 1 to 2-inch intervals between each scoop. Use the spoon to flatten the batter and cook until compacted and golden brown on the bottom part, 2 minutes.
3. Flip the hash brown and cook further for 2 minutes or until the vegetable cook and is golden brown. Transfer to a paper-towel-lined plate. Make the remaining hash browns using the remaining ingredients. Serve warm and enjoy!

Nutritional Value: Calories 286; Fat 18g; Carbohydrates 27.4g; Protein 8g

Recipe 25: Thyme Pumpkin Stir-Fry

Serving Size: 2

Cooking Time: 25 minutes

Ingredients:

- 1 cup pumpkin, shredded
- 1 tablespoon olive oil
- ½ onion, chopped
- 1 carrot, chopped
- 2 garlic cloves, minced
- ½ teaspoon dried thyme
- 1 cup chopped kale
- Sea salt and pepper to taste

Directions:

1. Heat the prepared olive oil in a skillet over medium heat.
2. Add and sauté the onion and carrot for 5 minutes, stirring often. Add in garlic and thyme, cook for 30 seconds until the garlic is fragrant.
3. Place in the pumpkin and cook for 10 minutes until tender.
4. Stir in kale, cook for 4 minutes until the kale wilts. Season with salt and pepper. Serve hot.

Nutritional Value: Calories 147; Fat 7g; Carbohydrates 10.7g; Protein 3.1g

Recipe 26: Tofu Scramble

Serving Size: 4

Cooking Time: 50 minutes

Ingredients:

- 8 oz extra firm tofu
- 2 tablespoon olive oil
- 1 red bell pepper, chopped
- 1 tomato, finely chopped
- 2 tablespoon chopped scallions
- Sea salt and pepper to taste
- 1 teaspoon red chili powder
- 3 teaspoon grated Parmesan cheese

Directions:

1. Place the tofu in between two parchment papers to drain liquid for about 30 minutes. Warm the prepared olive oil in a large nonstick skillet until no longer foaming. Crumble the tofu into the skillet and fry until golden brown, stirring occasionally, making sure not to break the tofu into tiny pieces, about 4 to 6 minutes.
2. Stir in the bell pepper, tomato, scallions, and cook until the vegetables are soft, about 4 minutes. Then, season with the prepared salt, pepper, chili powder, and stir in the Parmesan cheese to incorporate and melt for about 2 minutes. Spoon the scramble into a serving platter and serve.

Nutritional Value: Calories 130; Fat 11g; Carbohydrates 4.8g; Protein 7g

Recipe 27: Tomato and Avocado Omelet

Serving Size: 2

Cooking Time: 10 minutes

Ingredients:

- 2 eggs
- ¼ avocado, diced
- 4 cherry tomatoes, halved
- 1 tablespoon cilantro, chopped
- A squeeze lime juice
- Pinch of salt

Directions:

1. Put together the avocado, tomatoes, cilantro, lime juice, and salt in a small bowl, then mix well and set aside.
2. Warm a medium nonstick skillet on medium heat. Whisk the eggs until frothy and add to the pan. Move the eggs around gently with a rubber spatula until they begin to set.
3. Scatter the avocado mixture over half of the omelet. Remove from heat, and slide the omelet onto a plate as you fold it in half.
4. Serve immediately.

Nutritional Value: Calories 433; Fat 32.7g; Carbohydrates 10.6g; Protein 25.5g

Recipe 28: Turkey Scotch Eggs

Serving Size: 2

Cooking Time: 35 minutes

Ingredients:

- 1 clove garlic, chopped
- 4 eggs, boiled and peeled
- 16 oz ground turkey
- ½ teaspoon black pepper
- ½ teaspoon nutmeg
- ½ teaspoon cinnamon
- ½ teaspoon cloves
- ½ teaspoon dried tarragon
- ½ cup chopped parsley
- ½ tablespoon dried chives

Directions:

1. Place your oven to 375°F. Combine the turkey with the cinnamon, nutmeg, pepper, cloves, tarragon, chives, parsley, and garlic in a mixing bowl and mix with your hands until thoroughly mixed.
2. Divide the mixture into 4 circular shapes with the palms of your hands. Flatten each one into a pancake shape using the backs of your hands. Wrap the meat pancake around 1 egg until it's covered. Bake the Scotch Eggs in the oven for 25 minutes or until brown and crisp. Serve.

Nutritional Value: Calories 500; Fat 30g; Carbohydrates 4g; Protein 54g

Recipe 29: Turmeric Spice Pancakes

Serving Size: 4

Cooking Time: 10 minutes

Ingredients:

- 1/4 cup coconut flour sifted
- 1/2 teaspoon baking soda
- 1/2 teaspoon turmeric powder
- 1/2 teaspoon cinnamon powder
- 1/4 teaspoon ginger powder
- 1/4 teaspoon salt
- Pinch black pepper
- 3 eggs
- 1/4 cup unsweetened applesauce
- 1/4 cup milk of any kind
- 3 tablespoon coconut oil, ghee, or butter, melted
- 1 teaspoon vanilla extract
- Ghee, butter, or coconut oil for cooking
- Fruit and maple syrup for topping

Directions:

1. In a mixing bowl, whisk together the baking soda, flour, turmeric, cinnamon, ginger, salt, and pepper, and set to the side for now.
2. In a second bowl, beat together the applesauce, eggs, milk, butter (or whichever fat you are using), and vanilla.
3. Put the egg mixture into the flour mixture and mix until combined. The batter will be a bit thick.
4. In a huge skillet over medium-high heat, melt the coconut oil or butter. When it is hot, drop the batter into the skillet in whatever size pancakes you want.
5. Let them cook for around 2 minutes on each side. Repeat with remaining batter, adding more butter or oil if necessary.
6. Serve with fruit or maple syrup.

Nutritional Value: Calories 178; Fat 13g; Carbohydrates 8g; Protein 6g

Recipe 30: White and Green Quiche

Serving Size: 3

Cooking Time: 40 minutes

Ingredients:

- 3 cups fresh spinach, chopped
- 15 large free-range eggs
- 3 garlic cloves, minced
- 5 white mushrooms, sliced
- 1 small sized onion, finely chopped
- 1 ½ teaspoon baking powder
- Ground black pepper to taste
- 1 ½ cups coconut milk
- Ghee, as required to grease the dish
- Sea salt to taste

Directions:

1. Set the oven to 350°F.
2. Get a baking dish, then grease it with organic ghee.
3. Break all the eggs in a huge bowl, then whisk well.
4. Stir in coconut milk. Beat well
5. While you are whisking the eggs, start adding the remaining ingredients to them.
6. When all the ingredients are thoroughly blended, pour all of them into the prepared baking dish.
7. Bake for at least 40 minutes, up to the quiche is set in the middle. Enjoy!

Nutritional Value: Calories 608; Fat 53.4g; Carbohydrates 16.8g; Protein 20.2g

Chapter 4:   Lunch Recipes

Recipe 31: Baked Butternut Squash Rigatoni

Serving Size: 4

Cooking Time: 1 hour 30 minutes

Ingredients:

- 1 enormous butternut squash
- 3 garlic cloves
- 2 tablespoon olive oil
- 1 lb rigatoni
- ½ cup substantial cream
- 3 cups fontina cheese
- 2 tablespoon slashed crisp sage
- 1 tablespoon salt
- 1 teaspoon naturally ground pepper
- 1 cup panko breadcrumbs

Directions:

1. Preheat the broiler to 425°F. In the meantime, in a huge bowl, hurl squash, garlic, and olive oil to cover. Spot on a huge, rimmed preparing sheet and dish until delicate, around 60 minutes. Move the container to a wire rack and let cool marginally for around 10 minutes. Decrease stove to 350°F.
2. In the meantime, heat a huge pot of salted water to the point of boiling and cook rigatoni as per bundle bearings. Channel and put it in a safe spot.
3. Utilizing a blender or nourishment processor, purée held squash with overwhelming cream until smooth.
4. In a huge bowl, hurl squash puree withheld rigatoni, 2 cups fontina, savvy, salt, and pepper. Brush the base and sides of a 9-by 13-inch preparing dish with olive oil. Move the rigatoni-squash blend to the dish.
5. In a little bowl, consolidate the remaining fontina and panko. Sprinkle over pasta and heat until brilliant darker, 20 to 25 minutes.

Nutritional Value: Calories 654; Fat 47.9g; Carbohydrates 23.1g; Protein 34.4g

Recipe 32: Baked Swordfish with Cilantro and Pineapple

Serving Size: 4

Cooking Time: 20 minutes

Ingredients:

- 1 tablespoon coconut oil
- 2 pounds swordfish, or other firm white fish, cut into 2-inch pieces
- 1 cup pineapple chunks, fresh
- ¼ cup fresh cilantro, chopped
- 2 tablespoons fresh parsley, chopped
- 2 garlic cloves, minced
- 1 tablespoon coconut aminos
- 1 teaspoon salt
- ¼ teaspoon black pepper, freshly ground

Directions:

1. Preheat the oven to 400°F.
2. Grease a baking dish with the coconut oil.
3. Add the swordfish, pineapple, cilantro, parsley, garlic, coconut aminos, salt, and pepper to the dish and mix gently the ingredients together.
4. In the preheated oven, place the dish and bake for 15 to 20 minutes, or until the fish feels firm to the touch. Serve warm.

Nutritional Value: Calories 408; Fat 16g; Carbohydrates 7g; Protein 60g

Recipe 33: Balsamic Chicken and Beans

Serving Size: 4

Cooking Time: 40 minutes

Ingredients:

- 1 lb. trimmed fresh green beans
- ¼ c. balsamic vinegar
- 2 sliced shallots
- 2 tablespoons Red pepper flakes
- 4 skinless, de-boned chicken breasts
- 2 minced garlic cloves
- 3 tablespoons Extra virgin olive oil

Directions:

1. Combine 2 tablespoons of the prepared olive oil with the balsamic vinegar, garlic, and shallots. Pour it over the chicken breasts and refrigerate overnight.
2. The next day, preheat the oven to 375 0F.
3. Take the chicken out of the marinade and arrange in a shallow baking pan. Discard the rest of the marinade.
4. Bake in the oven for 40 minutes.
5. While the chicken is actually cooking, bring a large pot of water to a boil.
6. Place the green beans in the water and allow them to cook for five minutes and then drain.
7. Heat one tablespoon of olive oil in the pot and return the green beans after rinsing them.
8. Toss with red pepper flakes.

Nutritional Value: Calories 433; Fat 17.4g; Carbohydrates 12.9g; Protein 56.1g

Recipe 34: Blackened Chicken Breast

Serving Size: 2

Cooking Time: 15 minutes

Ingredients:

- 2 chicken breast halves, skinless and boneless
- 1 teaspoon thyme, ground
- 2 teaspoon paprika
- 2 teaspoon olive oil
- ½ teaspoon onion powder

Directions:

1. Combine the thyme, paprika, onion powder, and salt together in your bowl.
2. Transfer the spice mix to a flat plate.
3. Rub olive oil on the chicken breast. Coat fully.
4. Roll the chicken pieces in the spice mixture. Press down, ensuring that all sides have the spice mix.
5. Keep aside for 5 minutes.
6. In the meantime, preheat your air fryer to 360°F.
7. Keep the prepared chicken in the air fryer basket. Cook for 8 minutes.
8. Flip once and cook for another 7 minutes.
9. Transfer the breasts to a serving plate. Serve after 5 minutes.

Nutritional Value: Calories 424; Fat 11g; Carbohydrates 3g; Protein 79g

Recipe 35: Brisket with Blue Cheese

Serving Size: 6

Cooking Time: 8 hours 10 minutes

Ingredients:

- 1 cup of water
- 1/2 tablespoon garlic paste
- 1/4 cup soy sauce
- 1 ½ lb. corned beef brisket
- 1/3 teaspoon ground coriander
- 1/4 teaspoon cloves, ground
- 1 tablespoon olive oil
- 1 shallot, chopped
- 2 oz. blue cheese, crumbled
- Cooking spray

Directions:

1. Place a pan over moderate heat and add oil to heat.
2. Toss in shallots and stir and cook for 5 minutes.
3. Stir in garlic paste and cook for 1 minute.
4. Transfer it to the slow cooker, greased with cooking spray.
5. Place brisket in the same pan and sear until golden from both sides.
6. Transfer the beef to the slow cooker along with other ingredients except for cheese.
7. Put on its lid and cook for 8 hrs. on low heat.
8. Garnish with cheese and serve.

Nutritional Value: Calories 397; Fat 31.4g; Carbohydrates 39g; Protein 23.5g

Recipe 36: Chicken and Broccoli

Serving Size: 4

Cooking Time: 15 minutes

Ingredients:

- 2 minced garlic cloves
- 4 de-boned, skinless chicken breasts
- ½ c. coconut cream
- 1 tablespoon chopped oregano
- 2 c. broccoli florets
- 1 tablespoon organic olive oil
- 1 c. chopped red onions

Directions:

1. Heat up a pan while using the oil over medium-high heat, add chicken breasts and cook for 5 minutes on each side.
2. Add onions and garlic, stir and cook for 5 minutes more.
3. Add oregano, broccoli and cream, toss everything, cook for ten minutes more, divide between plates and serve.
4. Enjoy!

Nutritional Value: Calories 287; Fat 10g; Carbohydrates 14g; Protein 19g

Recipe 37: Chicken Breasts and Mushrooms

Serving Size: 6

Cooking Time: 25 minutes

Ingredients:

- 3 lb chicken breasts, skinless and boneless
- 1 yellow onion, chopped
- 1 garlic clove, minced
- A pinch of salt and black pepper
- 10 mushrooms, chopped
- 1 tablespoon olive oil
- 2 red bell peppers, chopped

Directions:

1. Put the prepared chicken in a baking dish, add onion, garlic, salt, pepper, mushrooms, oil and bell peppers. Mix briefly and bake in the oven at 425°F for 25 minutes.
2. Divide between plates and serve. Enjoy!

Nutritional Value: Calories 285; Fat 11g; Carbohydrates 13g; Protein 16g

Recipe 38: Chopped Lambs with Rosemary

Serving Size: 4

Cooking Time: 8 hours

Ingredients:

- 1 medium onion, sliced
- 2 teaspoon garlic powder
- 2 teaspoon rosemary, dried
- 1 teaspoon sea salt
- 1/2 teaspoon thyme leaves, dried
- Freshly ground black pepper
- 8 bone-in lamb chops, 3 lb
- 2 tablespoon balsamic vinegar

Directions:

1. Line the slow cooker's bottom with the onion slices.
2. Stir together the garlic powder, rosemary, salt, thyme, and pepper in a small bowl. Rub the chops evenly with the spice mixture and place gently in the slow cooker.
3. Drizzle the vinegar over the top.
4. Cover the cooker and set it to low. Cook for 7 to 8 hours and serve.

Nutritional Value: Calories 264; Fat 8.4g; Carbohydrates 10.3g; Protein 21.5g

Recipe 39: Cilantro-Lime Chicken Drumsticks

Serving Size: 6

Cooking Time: 15 minutes

Ingredients:

- ¼ cup fresh cilantro, chopped
- 3 tablespoons freshly squeezed lime juice
- ½ teaspoon garlic powder
- ½ teaspoon sea salt
- ¼ teaspoon ground cumin
- 3 pounds (1.4 kg) chicken drumsticks

Directions:

1. In a large-sized bowl, stir together the cilantro, lime juice, garlic powder, salt, and cumin to form a paste.
2. Put the drumsticks in the slow cooker. Spread the cilantro paste evenly on each drumstick.
3. Cover the cooker and set to high. Cook for approximately about 2 to 3 hours, or until the internal temperature of the chicken reaches 165°F (74°C) on a meat thermometer and the juices run clear, and serve.

Nutritional Value: Calories 417; Fat 12g; Carbohydrates 1g; Protein 7.1g

Recipe 40: Crusted Pork Chops

Serving Size: 4

Cooking Time: 20 minutes

Ingredients:

- ½ teaspoon salt
- ½ teaspoon onion powder
- 4 thick pork chops, center-cut boneless
- ¼ teaspoon pepper
- 1 teaspoon smoked paprika
- ¼ teaspoon chili powder
- 1 cup pork rind crumbs
- 2 large eggs
- 3 tablespoon Parmesan cheese, grated

Directions:

1. Prepare and preheat your Air fryer at 400 degrees F.
2. Rub the pork chops with black pepper and salt.
3. Whisk Parmesan cheese with seasonings and pork rind crumbs in a bowl.
4. Beat eggs in another bowl.
5. First, liberally dip the pork chops in the egg then coat them with cheese crumb mixture.
6. Place the prepared chops in the Air fryer basket and return the basket to the Air fryer.
7. Air fry for 20 minutes then serve.

Nutritional Value: Calories 271; Fat 12.3g; Carbohydrates 1.2g; Protein 38.5g

Recipe 41: Cumin Lamb Meatballs with Aioli

Serving Size: 4

Cooking Time: 30 minutes

Ingredients:

- 1 teaspoon ground cumin
- 2 tablespoon chopped cilantro
- 1 ½ lb ground lamb
- 1 tablespoon dried oregano
- 1 teaspoon onion powder
- 1 teaspoon garlic powder
- Sea salt and pepper to taste
- ½ cup garlic aioli

Directions:

1. Preheat your oven to 400°F.
2. Combine the ground lamb, cumin, cilantro, rosemary, oregano, onion powder, garlic powder, salt, and pepper in a bowl.
3. Shape 20 meatballs out of the mixture and transfer to a parchment-lined baking sheet.
4. Bake for 15 minutes until the meat reaches an internal temperature of 140°F.
5. Serve warm with aioli.

Nutritional Value: Calories 450; Fat 24g; Carbohydrates 11g; Protein 2g

Recipe 42: Garlic and Squash Noodles

Serving Size: 4

Cooking Time: 15 minutes

Ingredients:

For Preparing Sauce
- ¼ cup coconut milk
- 6 large dates
- 2/3 g gritted coconut
- 6 garlic cloves
- 2 tablespoons ginger paste
- 2 tablespoons red curry paste

For Preparing Noodles
- 1 large boil squash noodles
- ½ julienne cut carrots
- ½ julienne cut zucchini
- 1 small red bell pepper
- ¼ cup cashew nuts

Directions:

1. For making sauce, blend all the ingredients and make a thick puree.
2. Cut spaghetti squash lengthwise and make noodles.
3. Lightly brush the baking tray with olive oil and bake squash noodles at 40C for 5-6 minutes.
4. For serving, incorporate noodles and puree in a bowl. Or serve puree alongside the noodles.

Nutritional Value: Calories 405; Fat 28g; Carbohydrates 107g; Protein 7g

Recipe 43: Gingery Swordfish Kabobs

Serving Size: 4

Cooking Time: 35 minutes

Ingredients:

- 4 thick swordfish steaks, cubed
- ¾ cup sesame seeds
- Sea salt and pepper to taste
- ½ teaspoon ground ginger
- 2 tablespoon extra-virgin olive oil

Directions:

1. Preheat your oven to 400°F. In a large-sized shallow dish, combine the sesame seeds, salt, ground ginger, and pepper. In a medium bowl, toss the swordfish with the olive oil to coat.
2. Press the oiled cubes into the sesame seed mixture. Thread the cubes onto bamboo skewers. Place the skewers on a greased baking sheet. Bake them for 10-12 minutes, turning once halfway through. Serve and enjoy!

Nutritional Value: Calories 390; Fat 20g; Carbohydrates 7g; Protein 44g

Recipe 44: Honey-Balsamic Salmon and Lemon Asparagus

Serving Size: 4

Cooking Time: 10 minutes

Ingredients:

- 2 tablespoon balsamic vinegar
- 1 tablespoon raw honey
- 1 teaspoon sea salt, divided
- 1/2 teaspoon freshly ground black pepper
- 4 salmon filets (about 2 1/2 lb total)
- 1 1/2 cups water, divided
- 1 bunch asparagus, trimmed and halved
- 2 tablespoon ghee
- Juice of 1 lemon

Directions:

1. In a bowl, whisk the vinegar, honey, 1/2 teaspoon salt, and the pepper to combine. Drizzle the honey-vinegar mixture over the salmon, and using the back of the spoon, spread it evenly across the salmon.
2. Place a metal trivet or steam rack in the Instant Pot and pour in 1 cup of water. Place the salmon on the trivet, skin-side down. Lock the lid.
3. Select Pressure Cook mode and cook at high pressure for 3 minutes.
4. When cooking is complete, use a quick release.
5. Remove the lid. Using potholders, remove the trivet and salmon filets, transfer the fish to a serving platter or glass dish, and cover with aluminum foil. Set aside. Select Cancel.
6. Put the asparagus, the remaining 1/2 cup of water, the ghee, and the remaining 1/2 teaspoon salt into the Instant Pot. Lock the lid.
7. Select Pressure Cook mode and cook at high pressure for 2 minutes.
8. When cooking is complete, use a quick release.
9. Remove the lid and transfer the cooked asparagus to the serving platter with the fish.
10. Pour the lemon juice over the asparagus and fish and serve.

Nutritional Value: Calories 444; Fat 18g; Carbohydrates 11g; Protein 57g

Recipe 45: Honey-Roasted Chicken Thighs with Carrots

Serving Size: 4

Cooking Time: 50 minutes

Ingredients:

- 2 tablespoon unsalted butter, at room temperature
- 3 large carrots, thinly sliced
- 2 garlic cloves, minced
- 4 bone-in, skin-on chicken thighs
- 1 teaspoon salt
- ½ teaspoon dried rosemary
- ¼ teaspoon freshly ground black pepper
- 2 tablespoon honey
- 1 cup chicken broth or vegetable broth
- Lemon wedges, for serving

Directions:

1. Preheat the oven to 400°F. Grease the baking sheet with the butter.
2. Arrange the carrots and garlic in a single layer on the baking sheet.
3. Put the chicken, skin-side up, on top of the vegetables, and season with the salt, rosemary, and pepper.
4. Put the honey on top and add the broth.
5. Roast within 40 to 45 minutes. Remove, and then let it rest for 5 minutes, and serve with lemon wedges.

Nutritional Value: Calories 428; Fat 27g; Carbohydrates 15g; Protein 30g

Recipe 46: Juicy Broccolini with Anchovy Almonds

Serving Size: 6

Cooking Time: 10 minutes

Ingredients:

- 2 bunches of broccolini, trimmed
- 1 tablespoon extra-virgin olive oil
- 1 long fresh red chili, deseeded, finely chopped
- 2 garlic cloves, thinly sliced
- ¼ cup natural almonds, coarsely chopped
- 2 teaspoons lemon rind, finely grated
- A squeeze of lemon juice, fresh
- 4 anchovies in oil, chopped

Directions:

1. Warm the oil until hot in a large saucepan. Add the drained anchovies, garlic, chili, and lemon rind. Cook until aromatic, for 30 seconds, stirring frequently. Add the almond & continue to cook for a minute more, stirring frequently. Remove from the heat & add a squeeze of fresh lemon juice.
2. Then place the broccolini in a steamer basket set over a saucepan of simmering water. Cover & cook until crisp-tender, for 2 to 3 minutes. Drain well and then transfer to a large-sized serving plate. Top with the almond mixture. Enjoy.

Nutritional Value: Calories 350; Fat 7g; Carbohydrates 13g; Protein 6g

Recipe 47: Lemony Spanish Shrimp with Parsley

Serving Size: 2

Cooking Time: 20 minutes

Ingredients:

- 2 cups wild or basmati rice
- 4 cups of water
- 12 whole shrimp, peeled, deveined and the tails still intact
- 2 garlic cloves, crushed
- 1 white onion, diced
- 2 tablespoons extra virgin olive oil
- ½ teaspoon red pepper flakes
- 1 tablespoon parsley, crushed
- 1 lemon, juice and zest
- 1 lemon, cut into quarters

Directions:

1. Add the rice and 4 cups of water to a saucepan and boil on a high heat.
2. Lower the heat, and then cover and simmer for approximately about 15 minutes once boiling.
3. Heat the oil in a skillet on a medium heat and then sauté the onion, garlic and red pepper flakes for 5 minutes until soft and add the shrimp.
4. Sauté for approximately about 5 to 8 minutes or until shrimp is opaque.
5. Drain the rice and return to the heat for 3 minutes more with the lid on.
6. Add the rice to the shrimps.
7. Add in the parsley, zest and juice of 1 lemon and mix well.
8. Serve in a wide paella dish or a large serving dish. Scatter the lemon wedges around the edge and sprinkle with a little fresher parsley.
9. Season with black pepper to taste.

Nutritional Value: Calories 668; Fat 8g; Carbohydrates 130g; Protein 25g

Recipe 48: Mild Stir-Fried Baby Bok Choy

Serving Size: 6

Cooking Time: 15 minutes

Ingredients:

- 1 Tablespoon coconut oil
- 1 large onion, finely diced
- 1-inch piece fresh ginger, grated
- 1 Teaspoon cumin, ground
- 1 teaspoon turmeric, ground
- ½ teaspoon salt
- Baby bok choy heads, ends trimmed and sliced lengthwise
- 2 teaspoon Water
- 3 Cup brown rice, cooked

Directions:

1. Heat the prepared coconut oil in a large pan set over medium heat.
2. Add the onion and cook for 5 minutes.
3. Add the ginger, cumin, turmeric, and salt. Stir to coat the onion with the spices.
4. Add the bok choy. For 5 to 8 minutes, stir-fry until the bok choy is crisp-tender. Add 1 tablespoon of the prepared water at a time if the pan gets dry until done.
5. Serve with brown rice.

Nutritional Value: Calories 444; Fat 9g; Carbohydrates 76g; Protein 30g

Recipe 49: Miso Chicken with Sesame

Serving Size: 6

Cooking Time: 4 hours

Ingredients:

- ¼ cup white miso
- 2 tablespoons coconut oil, melted
- 2 tablespoons honey
- 1 tablespoon rice wine vinegar, unseasoned
- 2 garlic cloves, thinly sliced
- 1 teaspoon fresh ginger root, minced
- 1 cup chicken broth
- 8 boneless, skinless chicken thighs
- 2 scallions, sliced
- 1 tablespoon sesame seeds

Directions:

1. Combine the miso, coconut oil, honey, rice wine vinegar, garlic, and ginger root in a slow cooker. Mix it well.
2. Add the chicken and toss to combine. Cover and cook on high for approximately about 4 hours.
3. Transfer the chicken and sauce to a serving dish. Garnish with the scallions and sesame seeds and serve.

Nutritional Value: Calories 320; Fat 15g; Carbohydrates 17g; Protein 32g

Recipe 50: Mustardy Beef Steaks

Serving Size: 4

Cooking Time: 55 minutes

Ingredients:

- ½ cup olive oil
- 2 tablespoon Dijon mustard
- ½ cup balsamic vinegar
- 2 garlic cloves, minced
- 1 teaspoon rosemary, chopped
- 4 (½-inch thick) beef steaks
- Sea salt and pepper to taste

Directions:

1. Combine the olive oil, mustard, vinegar, garlic, rosemary, salt, and pepper in a bowl.
2. Add in steaks and toss to coat.
3. Let marinate covered for 30 minutes.
4. Remove any excess of the marinade from the steaks and transfer them to a warm skillet over high heat and cook for 4-6 minutes on both sides.
5. Let sit for 5 minutes and serve.

Nutritional Value: Calories 480; Fat 3g; Carbohydrates 4g; Protein 48g

Recipe 51: Pork with Cabbage and Kale

Serving Size: 4

Cooking Time: 35 minutes

Ingredients:

- 1-pound pork stew meat, cut into strips
- 2 tablespoons olive oil
- 1 yellow onion, chopped
- A pinch of salt and pepper
- cup green cabbage, shredded
- ½ cup baby kale
- 2 tablespoons oregano, dried
- 2 tablespoons balsamic vinegar
- ¼ cup vegetable stock

Directions:

1. Heat up a pan with the oil over medium-high heat, add the onion and the meat and brown for 5 minutes.
2. Add the cabbage and the other ingredients, toss gently and bake everything at 390 degrees F for 30 minutes.
3. Divide the whole mix between plates and serve.

Nutritional Value: Calories 331; Fat 18.7g; Carbohydrates 6.5g; Protein 34.2g

Recipe 52: Pork with Nutmeg Squash

Serving Size: 4

Cooking Time: 35 minutes

Ingredients:

- 1-pound pork stew meat, cubed
- 1 butternut squash, peeled and cubed
- 1 yellow onion, chopped
- 2 tablespoons olive oil
- 2 garlic cloves, minced
- ½ teaspoon garam masala
- ½ teaspoon nutmeg, ground
- 1 teaspoon chili flakes, crushed
- 1 tablespoon balsamic vinegar
- A pinch of salt and pepper

Directions:

1. Heat up a pan with the oil over medium-high heat, add the onion and the garlic and sauté for 5 minutes.
2. Add the meat and brown for another 5 minutes.
3. Add the rest of the ingredients, toss, cook over medium heat for 25 minutes, divide between plates and serve.

Nutritional Value: Calories 348; Fat 18.2g; Carbohydrates 11.4g; Protein 34.3g

Recipe 53: Rosemary Garlic Lamb Chops

Serving Size: 2

Cooking Time: 10 minutes

Ingredients:

- 4 chops lamb
- 1 teaspoon olive oil
- 2 teaspoon garlic puree
- Fresh garlic
- Fresh rosemary

Directions:

1. Keep your lamb chops in the fryer grill pan.
2. Season the chops with pepper and salt. Brush with some olive oil.
3. Add some garlic puree to each chop.
4. Cover the grill pan gaps with garlic cloves and rosemary sprigs.
5. Refrigerate to marinate.
6. Take out after 1 hour. Keep in the fryer and cook for 5 minutes.
7. Use your spatula to turn the chops over.
8. Add some olive oil and cook for another 5 minutes.
9. Set aside for a minute.
10. Take out the rosemary and garlic before serving.

Nutritional Value: Calories 678; Fat 37g; Carbohydrates 1g; Protein 83g

Recipe 54: Salmon and Asparagus Skewers

Serving Size: 8

Cooking Time: 10 minutes

Ingredients:

- 2 tablespoon ghee, melted
- 1 teaspoon Dijon mustard
- 1 teaspoon garlic powder
- 1/2 teaspoon salt
- 1/4 teaspoon red pepper flakes
- 1 1/2 lb boned skinless salmon, cut into 2-inch chunks
- 2 lemons, thinly sliced
- 1 bunch of asparagus spears, tough ends trimmed, cut into 2-inch pieces

Directions:

1. Preheat the broiler.
2. Line a baking sheet with aluminum foil.
3. In a prepared large-sized saucepan over medium heat, heat the ghee.
4. Stir in the mustard, garlic powder, salt, and red pepper flakes.
5. On each skewer, thread 1 chunk of salmon, 1 lemon slice folded in half, and 2 pieces of asparagus. Repeat with the remaining skewers until all ingredients are used. Place the skewers on the prepared pan and brush each with the ghee-seasoning mixture.
6. Broil for 4 minutes. Turn the skewers and broil on the other side for about 4 minutes.

Nutritional Value: Calories 250; Fat 9g; Carbohydrates 4g; Protein 4g

Recipe 55: Saucy Tropical Halibut

Serving Size: 4

Cooking Time: 35 minutes

Ingredients:

- ½ mango, diced
- 1 avocado, diced
- ½ cup chopped strawberries
- 1 teaspoon chopped fresh mint
- 1 lemon, juiced and zested
- 1 tablespoon olive oil
- 4 boneless, skinless halibut fillets
- Sea salt and pepper to taste

Directions:

1. Mix avocado, mango, strawberries, mint, lemon juice, and lemon zest in a bowl; stir well. Set the sauce aside.
2. Warm the prepared olive oil in a medium-sized pan over medium heat. Lightly season the prepared halibut with salt and pepper. Add the fish and fry for 3-4 minutes per side, turning once or until it is just cooked through. Top with avocado salsa and serve.

Nutritional Value: Calories 355; Fat 15g; Carbohydrates 12g; Protein 42g

Recipe 56: Seared Haddock with Beets

Serving Size: 4

Cooking Time: 30 minutes

Ingredients:

- 8 beets, peeled and cut into eighths
- 2 shallots, thinly sliced
- 2 tablespoons apple cider vinegar
- 2 tablespoons olive oil, divided
- 1 teaspoon bottled minced garlic
- 1 teaspoon chopped fresh thyme
- Pinch sea salt
- 4 (5-ounce / 142-g) haddock fillets, patted dry

Directions:

2. Preheat the oven to a heat of 400°F (205°C).
3. Combine the beets, shallots, vinegar, 1 tablespoon of olive oil, garlic, thyme, and sea salt in a medium bowl, and toss to coat well. Spread out the beet mixture in a baking dish.
4. Roast in the preheated oven for approximately about 30 minutes, turning once or twice with a spatula, or until the beets are tender.
5. Meanwhile, heat the remaining 1 tablespoon of the prepared olive oil in a large skillet over medium-high heat.
6. Add the haddock and sear each side for 4 to 5 minutes, or until the flesh is opaque and it flakes apart easily.
7. Transfer the fish to a plate and serve topped with the roasted beets.

Nutritional Value: Calories 343; Fat 8.8g; Carbohydrates 20.9g; Protein 38.1g

Recipe 57: Sesame-Tamari Baked Chicken with Green Beans

Serving Size: 4

Cooking Time: 45 minutes

Ingredients:

- 1 lb green beans, trimmed
- 4 bone-in, skin-on chicken breasts
- 2 tablespoon honey
- 1 tablespoon sesame oil
- 1 tablespoon gluten-free tamari or soy sauce
- 1 cup chicken or vegetable broth

Directions:

1. Preheat the oven to 400°F.
2. Arrange the green beans on a large rimmed baking sheet.
3. Put the chicken, skin-side up, on top of the beans.
4. Drizzle with honey, oil, and tamari. Add the broth.
5. Roast within 35 to 40 minutes. Remove, let it rest for 5 minutes and serve.

Nutritional Value: Calories 378; Fat 10g; Carbohydrates 19g; Protein 54g

Recipe 58: Spaghetti Bolognese

Serving Size: 8

Cooking Time: 20 minutes

Ingredients:

- 1 lb brown rice spaghetti
- 2 tablespoon ghee
- 3 garlic cloves, minced
- 1/2 cup chopped white onion
- 2/3 cup chopped celery
- 2/3 cup chopped carrot
- 1 lb lean ground beef
- 1 (15-oz) can of diced tomatoes with their juice
- 1 tablespoon white wine vinegar
- 1/2 teaspoon red pepper flakes
- 1/8 teaspoon ground nutmeg
- Dash salt
- Dash freshly ground black pepper

Directions:

1. Cook the spaghetti following the package instructions.
2. Meanwhile, in a large-sized skillet over medium heat, heat the ghee.
3. Add the prepared garlic and onion, and sauté for 5 minutes.
4. Add the celery and carrot, and sauté for 5 minutes. Push the vegetables to the side of the skillet.
5. Add the ground beef next to the vegetables. Sauté for 10 minutes, breaking up the meat as it begins to brown.
6. Stir in the tomatoes, vinegar, red pepper flakes, nutmeg, salt, and pepper, and bring to a simmer for 5 minutes.
7. Serve over the cooked noodles.

Nutritional Value: Calories 358; Fat 12g; Carbohydrates 48g; Protein 14g

Recipe 59: Turkey and Artichokes

Serving Size: 4

Cooking Time: 40 minutes

Ingredients:

- 1 yellow onion, sliced
- 1 pound turkey breast, skinless, boneless, and roughly cubed
- 1 Tablespoon olive oil
- Salt and black pepper to taste
- 1 cup of canned artichoke hearts, drained and halved
- ½ teaspoon nutmeg, ground
- ½ teaspoon sweet paprika
- 1 teaspoon cumin, ground
- 1 tablespoon cilantro, chopped

Directions:

1. In a roasting pan, combine the turkey with the onion, artichokes, and the other ingredients, toss and at 350°F for 40 minutes.
2. Divide everything between plates and serve.

Nutritional Value: Calories 345; Fat 12g; Carbohydrates 12g; Protein 14g

Recipe 60: Zucchini and Lemon Herb Salmon

Serving Size: 4

Cooking Time: 20 minutes

Ingredients:

- 2 tablespoon olive oil
- 4 chopped zucchinis
- 2 tablespoon lemon juice
- 2 tablespoon agave nectar
- 2 garlic cloves, minced
- 1 tablespoon Dijon mustard
- ½ teaspoon oregano, dried
- ½ teaspoon dill, dried
- ¼ teaspoon rosemary, dried
- ¼ teaspoon thyme, dried
- 4 salmon fillets
- 2 tablespoon parsley leaves, chopped
- Ground black pepper and kosher salt to taste

Directions:

1. Preheat your oven to 400°F.
2. Apply cooking spray on your baking sheet lightly.
3. Whisk together the lemon juice, brown sugar, dill, garlic, Dijon, rosemary, thyme, and oregano in a bowl.
4. Season with pepper and salt to taste. Set aside.
5. Keep the zucchini on your baking sheet in one single layer.
6. Drizzle some olive oil. Season with pepper and salt.
7. Add the fish in one layer. Brush each fillet with your herb mix.
8. Keep in the oven. Cook for 17 minutes.
9. Garnish with parsley and serve.

Nutritional Value: Calories 355; Fat 19g; Carbohydrates 15g; Protein 31g

Chapter 5:   Dinner Recipes

Recipe 61: Baked Tilapia with Chili Kale

Serving Size: 2

Cooking Time: 20 minutes

Ingredients:

- ½ cup whole-grain breadcrumbs
- ½ cup ground hazelnuts
- 2 tilapia fillets, skinless
- 2 teaspoon extra-virgin olive oil
- 2 teaspoon whole-grain mustard
- 5 oz kale, chopped
- 1 red chili, sliced
- 1 clove garlic, mashed

Directions:

1. Preheat your oven to 350ºF. Combine the hazelnuts and breadcrumbs in a bowl. Spread a thin layer of mustard over the fish and then dip into the breadcrumb mixture.
2. Transfer to a greased baking dish. Bake for 12 minutes or until cooked through.
3. Warm the prepared olive oil in a skillet over medium heat and sauté the garlic for 30 seconds. Add the kale and red chili and cook for 5 more minutes.
4. Serve fish with the kale on the side.

Nutritional Value: Calories 540; Fat 32g; Carbohydrates 29g; Protein 35g

Recipe 62: Chicken Lemon Piccata

Serving Size: 4

Cooking Time: 30 minutes

Ingredients:

- 2 chicken breasts, skinless & boneless
- 2 tablespoon dairy-free margarine
- 1 ½ tablespoon whole wheat flour
- ¼ teaspoon salt
- ¼ teaspoon white pepper
- ⅓ cup white wine, dry
- 2 tablespoon olive oil
- ¼ cup lemon juice
- ⅓ cup chicken stock, low-sodium
- ¼ cup minced Italian parsley
- ¼ cup capers, drained
- Pepper and salt to taste

Directions:

1. Cut in half each chicken breast. Spread your flour on a plate thinly. Season with pepper and salt. Dredge the breast slices lightly in your seasoned flour. Set aside.
2. Heat your sauté pan over medium temperature.
3. Add the breast slices to your pan when you see the oil simmering. Cook for 3 to 4 minutes.
4. Turn over the chicken slices. Take out the slices. Set aside.
5. Add wine to the pan. Stir. Scrape up those actually browned bits from the bottom.
6. Now add the chicken stock and lemon juice. Go to high heat. Boil till you have a thick sauce.
7. Bring down the heat. Stir the parsley and capers in.
8. Add back the breast slices to your pan. Rewarm.

Nutritional Value: Calories 227; Fat 15g; Carbohydrates 3g; Protein 20g

Recipe 63: Chipotle Trout with Spinach

Serving Size: 4

Cooking Time: 15 minutes

Ingredients:

- Extra-virgin olive oil, for brushing
- ½ red onion, thinly sliced
- 1 package frozen spinach, thawed
- 4 boneless trout fillets
- 1 teaspoon salt
- ¼ teaspoon chipotle powder
- ¼ teaspoon garlic powder
- 2 tablespoons fresh lemon juice

Directions:

1. Preheat the oven to a heat of 375°F (190°C). Brush a baking pan with olive oil.
2. Scatter the red onion and spinach in the pan.
3. Lay the trout fillets over the spinach.
4. Sprinkle the salt, chipotle powder, and garlic powder over the fish.
5. Cover with aluminum foil and bake until the trout is firm, about 15 minutes.
6. Drizzle with the lemon juice and serve.

Nutritional Value: Calories 160; Fat 7g; Carbohydrates 5g; Protein 19g

Recipe 64: Fiery Pork Loin with Lime

Serving Size: 6

Cooking Time: 7 hours

Ingredients:

- 3 teaspoon chili powder
- 2 teaspoon garlic powder
- 1 teaspoon cumin, ground
- 1/2 teaspoon sea salt
- 2 pork tenderloins, 1-lb
- 1 cup broth of choice
- 1/4 cup lime juice, freshly squeezed

Directions:

1. Stir together in a small bowl the chili powder, garlic powder, cumin, and salt. Rub the pork all over with the spice mixture and put it in the slow cooker.
2. Pour the broth and lime juice around the pork in the cooker.
3. Cover the cooker and set low. Cook for 6 to 7 hours.
4. Remove the pork and let rest for approximately about 5 minutes. Before serving, slice the pork against the grain into medallions.

Nutritional Value: Calories 240; Fat 2.2g; Carbohydrates 8.7g; Protein 23.9g

Recipe 65: Fried Haddock with Roasted Beets

Serving Size: 4

Cooking Time: 50 minutes

Ingredients:

- 4 peeled beets, cut into wedges
- 4 haddock fillets
- 2 shallots, thinly sliced
- 2 tablespoon apple cider vinegar
- 2 tablespoon olive oil, divided
- 1 teaspoon minced garlic
- 1 teaspoon chopped mint
- Sea salt to taste

Directions:

1. Preheat your oven to 400°F. Place the beets, shallots, vinegar, 1 tablespoon of olive oil, garlic, thyme, and sea salt in a medium bowl and toss to coat well. Spread out the beet mixture on a baking dish. Roast in the preheated oven for approximately about 30 minutes, turning once or twice with a spatula, or until the beets are tender.
2. Warm the remaining prepared olive oil in a large-sized skillet over medium heat. Add the haddock and sear each side for 4-5 minutes, or until the flesh is opaque and it flakes apart easily. Top with roasted beets.

Nutritional Value: Calories 340; Fat 9g; Carbohydrates 20g; Protein 37g

Recipe 66: Gingery Sea Bass

Serving Size: 2

Cooking Time: 15 minutes

Ingredients:

- 2 spring onions, sliced
- 2 sea bass fillets
- 1 teaspoon black pepper
- 1 tablespoon extra-virgin olive oil
- 1 teaspoon grated ginger
- 1 garlic clove, thinly sliced
- 1 red chili, thinly sliced
- 1 lime, zested

Directions:

1. Warm the prepared olive oil in a skillet over medium heat. Sprinkle black pepper over the fish and score the skin of the fish a few times with a sharp knife. Add the sea bass fillet to the skillet with the skin side down. Cook for 5 minutes and turn over. Cook for a further 2 minutes; reserve.
2. Add the chili, garlic, and ginger to the same skillet and cook for 2 minutes or until golden. Remove from the heat and add the spring onions. Scatter the vegetables and lime zest over your sea bass and serve.

Nutritional Value: Calories 205; Fat 10g; Carbohydrates 24g; Protein 5g

Recipe 67: Herby Green Whole Chicken

Serving Size: 6

Cooking Time: 1 hour 45 minutes

Ingredients:

- 1 sweet onion, quartered
- 1 whole chicken
- 2 lemons, halved
- 4 garlic cloves, crushed
- 4 fresh thyme sprigs
- 4 fresh rosemary sprigs
- 4 fresh parsley sprigs
- 3 bay leaves
- 2 tablespoon olive oil
- Sea salt and pepper to taste

Directions:

1. Preheat your oven to 400°F. Put the chicken in a greased pan.
2. Stuff it with lemons, onion, garlic, thyme, rosemary, parsley, and bay leaves into the cavity. Brush the chicken with prepared olive oil, and season lightly with sea salt and pepper.
3. Roast the chicken for about 1 ½ hours until golden brown and cooked through. Remove the prepared chicken from the oven and let it sit for 10 minutes.
4. Remove the lemons, onion, and herbs from the cavity and serve.

Nutritional Value: Calories 260; Fat 9g; Carbohydrates 39g; Protein 6g

Recipe 68: Hot and Spicy Shredded Chicken

Serving Size: 4

Cooking Time: 1 hour

Ingredients:

- 1 ½ lb boneless and skinless chicken breast
- 2 cups diced tomatoes
- ½ teaspoon oregano
- 2 green chilies, chopped
- ½ teaspoon paprika
- 2 tablespoon coconut sugar
- ½ cup salsa
- 1 teaspoon cumin
- 2 tablespoon olive oil

Directions:

1. In a large-sized bowl, combine the oil with all of the spices. Rub the chicken breast with the spicy marinade. Place the meat in your Instant Pot. Add the diced tomatoes.
2. Close the lid and cook for 25 minutes on "Manual". Transfer the chicken to a cutting board and shred it. Return the prepared shredded meat to the Instant Pot. Choose the "Slow Cook" setting and cook for 30 more minutes.

Nutritional Value: Calories 310; Fat 10g; Carbohydrates 12g; Protein 38g

Recipe 69: Hot Turkey Meatballs

Serving Size: 4

Cooking Time: 10 minutes

Ingredients:

- 1 pound turkey meat, ground
- 1 yellow onion, chopped
- 1 egg, whisked
- 1 tablespoon cilantro, chopped
- 1 Tablespoon olive oil
- 1 red chili pepper, minced
- 1 Teaspoon lime juice
- Zest of 1 lime, grated
- A pinch of salt and black pepper
- 1 teaspoon turmeric powder

Directions:

1. In a bowl, combine the turkey meat with the onion and the other ingredients except for the oil, stir & shape medium meatballs out of this mix.
2. Heat up a pan with the oil over medium-high heat, add the meatballs, cook them for 5 minutes on each side, divide between plates, and serve for dinner.

Nutritional Value: Calories 200; Fat 12g; Carbohydrates 12g; Protein 7g

Recipe 70: Lemon and Caper Turkey Scaloppine

Serving Size: 4

Cooking Time: 25 minutes

Ingredients:

- 1 tablespoon capers
- ¼ cup whole-wheat flour
- Sea salt and pepper to taste
- 4 turkey breast cutlets
- 2 tablespoon olive oil
- 3 lemons, juiced
- 1 lemon, zested
- 1 tablespoon chopped parsley

Directions:

1. Pound the prepared turkey with a rolling pin to ¼-inch thickness.
2. Combine the prepared flour, salt, and pepper in a bowl. Roll each cutlet piece in the flour, shaking off the excess. Warm the olive oil in a skillet over medium heat. Sear the cutlets for 4 minutes on both sides.
3. Transfer to a medium-sized plate and cover with aluminium foil.
4. Pour the lemon juice and lemon zest in the skillet to scrape up the browned bits that stick to the bottom of the skillet. Stir in capers and rosemary.
5. Cook for 2 minutes until the sauce has thickened slightly. Drizzle the sauce over the cutlets. Serve.

Nutritional Value: Calories 190; Fat 14g; Carbohydrates 9g; Protein 2g

Recipe 71: Lime Pork and Green Beans

Serving Size: 4

Cooking Time: 40 minutes

Ingredients:

- 2 pounds pork stew meat, cubed
- 2 tablespoons avocado oil
- ½ cup green beans, trimmed and halved
- 2 tablespoons lime juice
- 1 cup coconut milk
- 1 tablespoon rosemary, chopped
- A pinch of salt and black pepper

Directions:

1. Heat up a pan with the oil over medium heat, add the meat and brown for 5 minutes.
2. Add the rest of the ingredients, toss gently, bring to a simmer and cook over medium heat for 35 minutes more.
3. Divide the mix between plates and serve.

Nutritional Value: Calories 260; Fat 5g; Carbohydrates 9g; Protein 13g

Recipe 72: Miso Salmon and Green Beans

Serving Size: 4

Cooking Time: 25 minutes

Ingredients:

- 1 tablespoon sesame oil
- 1 lb green beans, trimmed
- 1 lb skin-on salmon fillets, cut into 4 steaks
- ¼ cup white miso
- 2 teaspoon gluten-free tamari or soy sauce
- 2 scallions, thinly sliced

Directions:

1. Preheat the oven to 400°F. Grease the baking sheet with the oil.
2. Put the green beans, then the salmon on top of the green beans, and brush each piece with the miso.
3. Roast within 20 to 25 minutes.
4. Drizzle with the tamari, sprinkle with the scallions and serve.

Nutritional Value: Calories 213; Fat 7g; Carbohydrates 13g; Protein 27g

Recipe 73: Mustard Pork Chops with Collard Greens

Serving Size: 4

Cooking Time: 25 minutes

Ingredients:

- 4 thin-cut pork chops
- Sea salt and pepper to taste
- 4 tablespoon Dijon mustard
- 3 tablespoon olive oil
- ½ red onion, finely chopped
- 4 cups chopped collard greens
- 2 tablespoon apple cider vinegar

Directions:

1. Preheat your oven to 425°F. Sprinkle pork chops with salt and pepper. Rub them with 2 tablespoon of mustard and transfer to a parchment-lined baking sheet. Bake for 15 minutes until the pork is cooked through.
2. Warm the olive oil in a large-sized skillet over medium heat. Add red onion and collard greens and cook for 7 minutes until soft. Combine the remaining mustard, apple cider vinegar, salt, and pepper in a bowl. Pour in the skillet and cook for 2 minutes. Serve the pork chops with kale side.

Nutritional Value: Calories 510; Fat 40g; Carbohydrates 11g; Protein 2g

Recipe 74: Parmesan and Lemon Fish

Serving Size: 2

Cooking Time: 10 minutes

Ingredients:

- 4 tilapia fillets
- ¼ cup cornflakes, crushed
- 2 tablespoon vegan Parmesan, grated
- 2 teaspoon vegan dairy-free butter, melted
- ⅛ teaspoon black pepper, ground
- ½ teaspoon lemon peel, shredded
- Lemon wedges

Directions:

1. Heat your oven to 450°F.
2. Rinse and then dry the fish using paper towels.
3. Apply cooking spray to your baking pan.
4. Now roll up your fish fillets. Start from their short ends.
5. Keep in the baking pan.
6. Bring together the vegan butter, Parmesan, cornflakes, pepper and lemon peel in a bowl.
7. Sprinkle the crumb mix on your fish roll-ups.
8. Press the crumbs lightly into the fish.
9. Bake for 6 to 8 minutes. The fish should flake easily with your fork.
10. Serve with lemon wedges.

Nutritional Value: Calories 191; Fat 7g; Carbohydrates 7g; Protein 25g

Recipe 75: Seared Trout with Greek Yogurt Sauce

Serving Size: 4

Cooking Time: 30 minutes

Ingredients:

- 1 garlic clove, minced
- 2 dill pickles, cubed
- ¼ cup Greek yogurt
- 3 tablespoon olive oil
- 4 trout fillets, patted dry
- 1 tablespoon olive oil
- Sea salt and pepper to taste

Directions:

1. Whisk yogurt, pickles, garlic, 1 tablespoon of olive oil, and salt in a small bowl. Set the sauce aside. Season the trout fillets lightly with salt and pepper.
2. Heat the remaining olive oil in a skillet over medium heat. Add the trout fillets to the hot skillet and panfry for about 10 minutes, flipping the fish halfway through or until the fish is cooked to your liking. Spread the salsa on top of the fish and serve.

Nutritional Value: Calories 325; Fat 15g; Carbohydrates 5g; Protein 38g

Recipe 76: Shrimp and Egg Risotto

Serving Size: 6

Cooking Time: 40 minutes

Ingredients:

- 4 cups water
- 4 garlic cloves, minced
- 2 eggs, beaten
- ½ teaspoon grated ginger
- 3 tablespoon olive oil
- ¼ teaspoon cayenne pepper
- 1 ½ cups frozen peas
- 2 cups brown rice
- ¼ cup soy sauce
- 1 cup chopped onion
- 12 oz peeled shrimp, thawed

Directions:

1. Heat the prepared olive oil in your Instant Pot on "Sauté". Add the prepared onion and garlic and cook for 2 minutes. Stir in the remaining ingredients except for the shrimp and eggs.
2. Close the lid and cook on "Manual" for 20 minutes. Wait about 10 minutes before doing a quick release. Stir in the shrimp and eggs. And let them heat for approximately about a couple of seconds with the lid off. Serve and enjoy!

Nutritional Value: Calories 220; Fat 10g; Carbohydrates 20g; Protein 13g

Recipe 77: Shrimp-Lime Bake with Zucchini and Corn

Serving Size: 4

Cooking Time: 20 minutes

Ingredients:

- 1 tablespoon extra-virgin olive oil
- 2 small zucchinis, cut into ¼-inch dice
- 1 cup frozen corn kernels
- 2 scallions, thinly sliced
- 1 teaspoon salt
- ½ teaspoon ground cumin
- ½ teaspoon chipotle chili powder
- 1 lb peeled shrimp, thawed if necessary
- 1 tablespoon finely chopped fresh cilantro
- Zest and juice 1 lime

Directions:

1. Preheat the oven to 400°F. Grease the baking sheet with the oil.
2. On the baking sheet, combine the zucchini, corn, scallions, salt, cumin, and chili powder and mix well. Arrange in a single layer.
3. Add the shrimp on top. Roast within 15 to 20 minutes.
4. Put the cilantro and lime zest and juice, stir to combine, and serve.

Nutritional Value: Calories 184; Fat 5g; Carbohydrates 11g; Protein 26g

Recipe 78: Shrimp with Zucchini

Serving Size: 4

Cooking Time: 20 minutes

Ingredients:

- 1 pound shrimp, peeled and deveined
- 1 tablespoon lemon juice
- 2 Zucchinis, sliced
- 1 yellow onion, roughly chopped
- 1 tablespoon olive oil
- 1 teaspoon turmeric powder
- A pinch of salt and black pepper
- 1 tablespoon capers, drained
- 1 Tablespoon pine nuts

Directions:

1. Heat a pan with the oil over medium-high heat, add the onion and the zucchini, stir and sauté for 5 minutes.
2. Add the shrimp & the other ingredients, toss, cook everything for 12 minutes more, divide into bowls and serve for lunch.

Nutritional Value: Calories 162; Fat 3g; Carbohydrates 12g; Protein 7g

Recipe 79: Smoked Trout Wrapped in Lettuce

Serving Size: 4

Cooking Time: 45 minutes

Ingredients:

- ¼ cup salt-roasted potatoes
- 1 cup grape tomatoes
- ½ cup basil leaves
- 16 small & medium size lettuce leaves
- 1/3 cup asian sweet chili
- 2 carrots
- 1/3 cup shallots (thin sliced)
- ¼ cup thin slice jalapenos
- 1 tablespoon sugar
- 2-4.5 ounces skinless smoked trout
- 2 tablespoon fresh lime juice
- 1 cucumber

Directions:

1. Cut carrots and cucumber in slim strip size.
2. Marinate these vegetables for 20 mins with sugar, fish sauce, lime juice, shallots, and jalapeno.
3. Add trout pieces and other herbs in this vegetable mixture and blend.
4. Strain water from vegetable and trout mixture and again toss it to blend.
5. Place lettuce leaves on a plate and transfer trout salad on them.
6. Garnish this salad with peanuts and chili sauce.

Nutritional Value: Calories 180; Fat 12g; Carbohydrates 18g; Protein 12g

Recipe 80: Smoky Lamb Souvlaki

Serving Size: 4

Cooking Time: 25 minutes

Ingredients:

- 1 lb lamb shoulder, cubed
- 2 tablespoon olive oil
- 1 tablespoon apple cider vinegar
- 2 teaspoon crushed fennel seeds
- 2 teaspoon smoked paprika
- Salt and garlic powder to taste

Directions:

1. Blend the olive oil, cider vinegar, crushed fennel seeds, smoked paprika, garlic powder, and sea salt in a large bowl. Stir in the lamb.
2. Cover the large-sized bowl and refrigerate it for 1 hour to marinate.
3. Preheat a frying pan over high heat. Thread 4-5 pieces of lamb each onto 8 skewers.
4. Fry for 3-4 minutes per side until cooked through. Serve.

Nutritional Value: Calories 275; Fat 15g; Carbohydrates 13g; Protein 31g

Recipe 81: Spicy Beef Fajitas

Serving Size: 4

Cooking Time: 15 minutes

Ingredients:

- 1 ½ lb flank steak, cut into strips
- ½ teaspoon ancho chili powder
- 3 tablespoon olive oil
- 2 green bell peppers, sliced
- 1 onion, sliced
- 1 cup store-bought salsa
- 1 teaspoon garlic powder
- ½ teaspoon Fajita seasoning

Directions:

1. Warm the prepared olive oil in a skillet over medium heat.
2. Stir-fry the flank steak strips, bell peppers, and onion for 6 minutes until browned.
3. Stir in ancho chili powder, salsa, garlic powder, and fajita seasoning and cook for 3 minutes, stirring often.
4. Serve right away.

Nutritional Value: Calories 480; Fat 26g; Carbohydrates 13g; Protein 3g

Recipe 82: Spicy Lime Pork Tenderloins

Serving Size: 4

Cooking Time: 7 hours 15 minutes

Ingredients:

- 2 lb pork tenderloins
- 1 cup chicken broth
- ¼ cup lime juice
- 3 teaspoon chili powder
- 2 teaspoon garlic powder
- 1 teaspoon ginger powder
- ½ teaspoon sea salt

Directions:

1. Combine chili powder, garlic powder, ginger powder, and salt in a bowl.
2. Rub the prepared pork all over with the spice mixture and put it in your slow cooker.
3. Pour in the broth and lime juice around the pork. Cover with the lid and cook for 7 hours on "Low".
4. Remove the pork from the slow cooker and let rest for 5 minutes. Slice the pork against the grain into medallions before serving.

Nutritional Value: Calories 260; Fat 6g; Carbohydrates 49g; Protein 5g

Recipe 83: Thyme Shark Steaks with Worcestershire

Serving Size: 2

Cooking Time: 40 minutes

Ingredients:

- 2 shark steaks, skinless
- 2 tablespoons onion powder
- 2 teaspoons chili powder
- 1 garlic clove, minced
- ¼ cup Worcestershire sauce
- 1 tablespoon ground black pepper
- 2 tablespoons thyme, chopped

Directions:

1. In a bowl, mix all the seasonings and spices to form a paste before setting aside.
2. Spread a thin layer of paste on both sides of the fish, cover and chill for 30 minutes (If possible).
3. Preheat the oven to 325°F (163°C).
4. Bake the fish in parchment paper for 30-40 minutes, until well cooked.
5. Serve on a bed of quinoa or wholegrain couscous and your favorite salad.

Nutritional Value: Calories 292; Fat 8g; Carbohydrates 17g; Protein 37g

Recipe 84: Trout and Salsa

Serving Size: 2

Cooking Time: 20 minutes

Ingredients:

- 2 trout fillets, boneless
- ½ cup chopped yellow onion
- 4 teaspoon olive oil
- 1 teaspoon minced garlic
- 1 green bell pepper, chopped
- ½ cup canned tomato salsa
- 2 tablespoon kalamata olives, pitted and chopped
- ¼ cup chicken stock
- A pinch of salt and black pepper

Directions:

1. Heat up a pan with 2 teaspoon oil over medium heat, add bell pepper and onion then stir and cook for 3 minutes. Add garlic, stock, olives and salsa, stir, cook for 5 minutes and transfer to a bowl.
2. Heat up the pan again with the rest of the oil over medium heat, add fish, season with salt and pepper and cook for 2 minutes on each side. Transfer to a baking dish, pour the salsa over the fish and place in the oven to bake at 425°F for 6 minutes. Divide between plates and serve.
3. Enjoy!

Nutritional Value: Calories 200; Fat 5g; Carbohydrates 12g; Protein 12g

Recipe 85: Trout Fillets with Chard and Raisins

Serving Size: 4

Cooking Time: 15 minutes

Ingredients:

- 4 boneless trout fillets
- Salt
- Freshly ground black pepper
- 1 tablespoon extra-virgin olive oil
- 1 onion, chopped
- 2 garlic cloves, minced
- 2 bunches chard, sliced
- ¼ cup golden raisins
- 1 tablespoon apple cider vinegar
- ½ cup vegetable broth

Directions:

1. Preheat the oven to a heat of 375°F (190°C).
2. Season the trout with salt and pepper.
3. In a large oven-proof pan over medium-high heat, heat the olive oil. Add the onion and garlic. Sauté for 3 minutes; add the chard and sauté for 2 minutes more.
4. Add the raisins, cider vinegar, and broth to the pan. Layer the trout fillets on top. Cover the large-sized pan and place it in the preheated oven for about 10 minutes, or until the trout is cooked through.

Nutritional Value: Calories 231; Fat 10g; Carbohydrates 13g; Protein 24g

Recipe 86: Tuna Steaks

Serving Size: 2

Cooking Time: 15 minutes

Ingredients:

- 1 ½ cup water
- 1 tablespoon lemon juice
- Pepper and salt to taste
- 1 teaspoon cayenne pepper
- 2 tuna steaks
- 3 kumquats, seeded, sliced, rinsed
- ⅓ cup cilantro, chopped

Directions:

1. Mix lemon juice, cayenne pepper and water over medium heat in a saucepan.
2. Season with pepper and salt. Boil.
3. Now include the tuna steaks into this mix.
4. Sprinkle cilantro and kumquats.
5. Cook for 15 minutes. The fish should flake easily with your fork.

Nutritional Value: Calories 141; Fat 1g; Carbohydrates 6g; Protein 27g

Recipe 87: Vegetable and Chicken Stir Fry

Serving Size: 6

Cooking Time: 15 minutes

Ingredients:

- 3 tablespoon olive oil
- 3 chicken breasts
- 3 medium zucchini or yellow squash
- 2 onions
- 1 teaspoon garlic powder
- 1 broccoli
- 1 teaspoon basil
- 1 teaspoon pepper and salt

Directions:

1. Chop the vegetables and chicken.
2. Heat your skillet over medium temperature.
3. Pour olive oil and add the chicken. Cook while stirring.
4. Include the seasonings if you want.
5. Add the vegetables. Keep cooking until it gets slightly soft. Add the onions first and broccoli last.

Nutritional Value: Calories 183; Fat 11g; Carbohydrates 9g; Protein 12g

Recipe 88: Veggie and Beef Brisket

Serving Size: 4

Cooking Time: 55 minutes

Ingredients:

- 4 beef tenderloin fillets
- 4 sweet potatoes, chopped
- 1 onion, chopped
- 2 bay leaves
- 2 tablespoon olive oil
- 2 cups chopped carrots
- 3 tablespoon chopped garlic
- 3 tablespoon Worcestershire sauce
- 2 celery stalks, chopped
- Black pepper to taste
- 1 tablespoon Knorr demi-glace sauce

Directions:

1. Heat 1 tablespoon oil in your pressure cooker on "Sauté". Sauté the onion until caramelized. Transfer to a bowl. Season the meat with pepper to taste. Heat the remaining oil and cook the meat until browned on all sides. Add the remaining ingredients and 2 cups of water. Close the cover lid and cook for 30 minutes on "Manual" on High pressure.
2. When cooking is complete, release the pressure naturally for 10 minutes. Transfer the meat and veggies to a serving platter. Whisk the Knorr Demi-Glace sauce in the pot and simmer for 5 minutes until thickened on "Sauté". Pour the prepared gravy over the meat and enjoy.

Nutritional Value: Calories 400; Fat 20g; Carbohydrates 10g; Protein 28g

Recipe 89: Wasabi-Ginger Salmon Burgers

Serving Size: 2

Cooking Time: 10 minutes

Ingredients:

- ½ teaspoon honey
- 2 tablespoons reduced-salt soy sauce
- 1 teaspoon wasabi powder
- 1 beaten free range egg
- 2 cans wild salmon, drained
- 2 scallions, chopped
- 2 tablespoons coconut oil
- 1 tablespoon fresh ginger, minced

Directions:

1. Combine the salmon, egg, ginger, scallions and 1 tablespoon oil in a bowl, mixing well with your hands to form 4 patties.
2. In a separate bowl, add the wasabi powder and soy sauce with the honey and whisk until blended.
3. Heat 1 tablespoon oil over medium heat in a skillet and cook the patties for 4 minutes on each side until firm and browned.
4. Glaze the top of each patty with the wasabi mixture and cook for another 15 seconds before you serve.
5. Serve with your actual favorite side salad or vegetables for a healthy treat.

Nutritional Value: Calories 553; Fat 30g; Carbohydrates 68g; Protein 4g

Recipe 90: Worcestershire Pork Chops

Serving Size: 6

Cooking Time: 35 minutes

Ingredients:

- 1 onion, diced
- 8 pork chops
- ¼ cup olive oil
- 3 tablespoon Worcestershire sauce
- 4 sweet potatoes, diced

Directions:

1. Heat half of the oil in your pressure cooker on "Sauté". Brown the pork chops on all sides and season with salt and pepper. Set aside.
2. Add the rest of the oil to the Instant Pot. Add onions and sauté for 2 or 3 minutes. Add potatoes and add 1 cup of water and Worcestershire sauce. Return the pork chops to the cooker. Close the lid, press "Manual" and cook for 15 minutes. When cooking is complete, select Cancel and perform a natural pressure release. This will take about 15 minutes.

Nutritional Value: Calories 785; Fat 40g; Carbohydrates 26g; Protein g

Chapter 6:   Dessert Recipes

Recipe 91: Banana Ginger Bars

Serving Size: 5

Cooking Time: 40 minutes

Ingredients:

- 2 large ripe bananas, peeled and mashed
- 1 cup coconut flour
- 1/3 cup coconut oil
- 1/3 cup raw honey
- 6 eggs, pasture-raised
- 1 tablespoon grated fresh ginger
- 2 teaspoons cinnamon powder
- 1 teaspoon ground cardamom powder
- 1 teaspoon baking soda
- 2 teaspoons apples cider vinegar

Directions:

1. Preheat the oven to 3500F. Grease a baking dish.
2. Combine the bananas, coconut flour, coconut oil, honey, eggs, ginger, cinnamon, and cardamom in a food processor. Pulse until smooth.
3. Put the baking soda plus apple cider vinegar last and quickly blend.
4. Pour into the prepared pan. Bake within 40 minutes. Allow cooling before slicing.

Nutritional Value: Calories 364; Fat 26g; Carbohydrates 23g; Protein 12g

Recipe 92: Chocolate Campanelle with Hazelnuts

Serving Size: 4

Cooking Time: 10 minutes

Ingredients:

- ½ cup chopped toasted hazelnuts
- ¼ cup dark chocolate chips
- 8 oz campanelle pasta
- 3 tablespoon almond butter
- ¼ cup maple syrup

Directions:

1. Pulse the hazelnuts and chocolate pieces in a food processor until crumbly. Set aside. Place the campanelle pasta in a pot with boiling salted water.
2. Cook for 8-10 minutes until al dente, stirring often. Drain and back to the pot. Stir in almond butter and maple syrup and stir until the butter is melted.
3. Serve garnished with chocolate-hazelnut mixture.

Nutritional Value: Calories 360; Fat 20g; Carbohydrates 44g; Protein 4g

Recipe 93: Dark Chocolate Granola Bars

Serving Size: 12

Cooking Time: 25 minutes

Ingredients:

- 1 cup tart cherries, dried
- 2 cups buckwheat
- ¼ cup flaxseed
- 1 cup walnuts
- 2 eggs
- 1 teaspoon salt
- ¼ cup dark cocoa powder
- ⅔ cup honey
- ½ cup dark chocolate chips
- 1 teaspoon vanilla

Directions:

1. Preheat your oven to 350°F.
2. Apply cooking spray lightly to your baking pan.
3. Pulse together the walnuts, wheat, tart cherries, salt, and flaxseed in your food processor. Everything should be chopped fine.
4. Whisk together the honey, eggs, vanilla, and cocoa powder in a bowl.
5. Add the wheat mix to your bowl. Stir to combine well.
6. Include the chocolate chips. Stir again.
7. Now pour this mixture into your baking dish.
8. Sprinkle some chocolate chips and tart cherries.
9. Bake for 25 minutes. Set aside for cooling before serving.

Nutritional Value: Calories 634; Fat 27g; Carbohydrates 100g; Protein 9g

Recipe 94: Hazelnut Topped Caramelized Bananas

Serving Size: 4

Cooking Time: 15 minutes

Ingredients:

- 2 bananas, peeled, halved crosswise and then lengthwise
- 2 tablespoon coconut oil
- 2 tablespoon coconut sugar
- 2 tablespoon spiced apple cider
- 2 chopped hazelnuts

Directions:

1. Warm the coconut oil in a large-sized skillet over medium heat.
2. Fry the bananas for 4 minutes, turning once.
3. Pour the sugar and cider around the bananas, cook for 2-3 minutes, until thickens and caramelize.
4. Remove to a serving plate and pour the cooked sauce over. Serve topped with hazelnuts.

Nutritional Value: Calories 315; Fat 25g; Carbohydrates 24g; Protein 5g

Recipe 95: Mint Chocolate Chip Ice Cream

Serving Size: 2

Cooking Time: 0 minutes

Ingredients:

- 2 frozen overripe bananas
- Pinch spirulina or any natural food coloring, optional.
- 3 tablespoon chocolate chips or sugar-free chocolate chips
- ⅛ teaspoon pure peppermint extracts
- ½ cup raw cashews or coconut cream, optional.
- Pinch Salt

Directions:

1. Mint or imitation peppermint won't be a substitute for this. Use pure peppermint extract and pour it all at once because a drop is more potent than you realize, so add slowly.
2. Peel and cut the bananas first. Place the slices in a Ziplock bag, then freeze.
3. For the ice cream, put all the ingredients in a blender and pulse. You can skip the chocolate chips and just add them after blending. It'll turn out delicious either way.
4. Serve as soon as it's ready or freeze until it's firm enough, then serve!

Nutritional Value: Calories 250; Fat 24.3g; Carbohydrates 7.7g; Protein 6.1g

Recipe 96: Sherbet Pineapple

Serving Size: 4

Cooking Time: 0 minutes

Ingredients:

- 1 can of 8 oz pineapple chunks
- ¼ teaspoon ground ginger
- ¼ teaspoon vanilla extract
- 1 can 11 oz orange sections
- 2 cups pineapple, lemon or lime sherbet
- ⅓ cup orange marmalade

Directions:

1. Drain the pineapple, and ensure you reserve the juice.
2. Take a moderate-sized container and put pineapple juice, ginger, vanilla and marmalade into the container
3. Put in pineapple chunks, drained mandarin oranges as well
4. Toss thoroughly and coat everything
5. Free them for 15 minutes and let them chill
6. Ladle the sherbet into 4 chilled stemmed sherbet dishes
7. Top each of them with a fruit mixture
8. Enjoy!

Nutritional Value: Calories 267; Fat 1g; Carbohydrates 65g; Protein 2g

Recipe 97: Spiced Tea Pudding

Serving Size: 3

Cooking Time: 10 minutes

Ingredients:

- ½ cup coconut flakes
- ½ teaspoon cloves
- 1(½) cup berries
- 1 can coconut milk
- 1 cup almond milk
- 1 tablespoon chia seeds
- 1 tablespoon ground cinnamon
- 1 tablespoon raw honey
- 1 teaspoon allspice
- 1 teaspoon cardamom
- 1 teaspoon green tea powder
- 1 teaspoon nutmeg
- ½ Tablespoon pumpkin seeds
- 1 Teaspoon ground ginger

Directions:

1. In your blender, puree tea powder with coconut milk, almond milk, cinnamon, coconut flakes, nutmeg, allspice, cloves, honey, cardamom, and ginger split into bowls.
2. Heat a pan on moderate heat, put in berries until bubbling, then move to your blender and pulse well. Split the berries into the bowls with the coconut milk mix. Top with chia seeds and pumpkin seeds before you serve. Enjoy!

Nutritional Value: Calories 150; Fat 6g; Carbohydrates 14g; Protein 8g

Recipe 98: Strawberry Granita

Serving Size: 8

Cooking Time: 10 minutes

Ingredients:

- 13 Pound strawberries, halved & hulled
- 1 cup of water
- Agave to taste
- ¼ teaspoon balsamic vinegar
- ½ teaspoon lemon juice
- Just a small pinch of salt

Directions:

1. Rinse the strawberries in water.
2. Keep in a blender. Add water, agave, balsamic vinegar, salt, and lemon juice.
3. Pulse the mixture several times to get it moving. To make it smooth, combine all the ingredients into a blender.
4. Fill a baking dish halfway with the mixture. The purée should only be 3/8 inch thick.
5. Cover the dish and place it in the refrigerator until the edges begin to freeze. Slushy should be in the center.
6. Lightly stir crystals from the edges into the middle. Make a thorough mix.
7. Chill the granite until it is nearly frozen.
8. Scrape the crystals loose and combine as previously.
9. Refrigerate once more. 3-4 times with a fork, mix until the granite is light.

Nutritional Value: Calories 238; Fat 28g; Carbohydrates 10g; Protein 5g

Recipe 99: Vanilla Cranberry and Almond Balls

Serving Size: 6

Cooking Time: 25 minutes

Ingredients:

- 2 tablespoon almond butter
- 2 tablespoon maple syrup
- ¾ cup cooked millet
- ¼ cup sesame seeds
- 1 tablespoon chia seeds
- ½ teaspoon almond extract
- Zest of 1 orange
- 1 tablespoon dried cranberries
- ¼ cup ground almonds

Directions:

1. Whisk the almond butter and syrup in a bowl until creamy.
2. Mix in millet, sesame seeds, chia seeds, almond extract, orange zest, cranberries, and almonds.
3. Shape the mixture into balls and arrange on a parchment paper-lined baking sheet.
4. Let chill in the fridge for 15 minutes.

Nutritional Value: Calories 120; Fat 8g; Carbohydrates 11g; Protein 2g

Recipe 100:   Walnut Chocolate Squares

Serving Size: 6

Cooking Time: 10 minutes

Ingredients:

- 4 oz dark chocolate
- 4 tablespoon peanut butter
- 1 pinch of sea salt
- ¼ cup walnut butter
- ½ teaspoon vanilla extract
- ¼ cup chopped walnuts

Directions:

1. Pour the chocolate and peanut butter into a safe microwave bowl and melt in the microwave for 1-2 minutes.
2. Remove the bowl from the microwave and mix in salt, walnut butter, and vanilla. Pour the batter into a greased baking dish and use a spatula to spread out into a rectangle.
3. Top with walnuts and chill in the refrigerator. Once set, cut into squares. Serve while firming.

Nutritional Value: Calories 245; Fat 26g; Carbohydrates 2g; Protein 2g

Chapter 7: 28-Day Meal Plan

Day	Breakfast	Lunch	Dinner
1	Ham and Veggie Frittata Muffins	Sesame-Tamari Baked Chicken with Green Beans	Baked Tilapia with Chili Kale
2	Hash Browns	Saucy Tropical Halibut	Lime Pork and Green Beans
3	Oatmeal Pancakes	Chicken and Broccoli	Smoky Lamb Souvlaki
4	Baked Eggs with Portobello Mushrooms	Lemony Stir-Fried Baby Bok Choy	Lemon and Caper Turkey Scaloppine
5	Scotch Eggs with Ground Turkey	Baked Swordfish and Cilantro and Pineapple	Smoked Trout Wrapped in Lettuce
6	White and Green Quiche	Ginger Swordfish Kabobs	Hot Turkey Meatballs
7	Turkey Scotch Eggs	Seared Haddock with Beets	Tuna Steaks
8	Coconut Porridge with Strawberries	Baked Butternut Squash Rigatoni	Miso Salmon and Green Beans
9	Salmon and Egg Scramble	Crusted Pork Chops	Spicy Beef Fajitas
10	Spicy Quinoa	Gingery Swordfish Kabobs	Chicken Lemon Piccata
11	Lemon-Almond Waffles	Balsamic Chicken and Beans	Parmesan and Lemon Fish
12	Spinach Breakfast	Miso Chicken with Sesame	Trout and Salsa
13	Scrambled Tofu with Bell Pepper	Honey-Roasted Chicken Thighs with Carrots	Mustard Pork Chops with Collard Greens
14	Beef Breakfast Casserole	Spaghetti Bolognese	Chipotle Trout with Spinach
15	Tofu Scramble	Cumin Lamb Meatballs with Aioli	Spicy Lime Pork Tenderloins
16	Crispy Chicken Fingers	Chicken and Broccoli	Shrimp with Zucchini
17	Qyinoa and Cauliflower	Zucchini and Lemon Herb	Hot and Spicy Shredded

	Congee	Salmon	Chicken
18	Blueberry Sweet Potato Bakfast Meatballs	Mild Stir-Fried Baby Bok Choy	Seared Trou with Greek Yogurt Sauce
19	Scrambled Eggs with Smoked Salmon	Chopped Lambs with Rosemary	Trout Fillets with Chard and Raisins
20	Turmeric Spince Pancakes	Brisket with Blue Cheese	Fiery Pork Loin with Lime
21	Oregano Scramble with Cherry Tomatoes	Juicy Broccolini with Anchovy Almonds	Thyme Shark Steaks with Worcestershire
22	Thyme Pumpkin Stir-Fry	Mustardy Beef Steaks	Veggie and Beef Brisket
23	Blueberry-Topped Steel-Cut Oats	Honey-Balsamic Salmon and Lemon Asparagus	Fried Haddock with Roasted Beets
24	Spicy Marble Eggs	Blackened Chicken Breast	Shrimp and Egg Risotto
25	Tomato and Avocado Omelet	Sesame-Tamari Baked Chicken with Green Beans	Herby Green Whole Chicken
26	Buckwheat and Chia Seed Overnight Oats	Baked Swordfish with Cilantro and Pineapple	Wasabi-Ginger Salmon Burgers
27	Breakfast Spinach Mushroom Tomato Fry Up	Chicken Breasts and Mushrooms	Shrimp-Lime Bake with Zucchini and Corn
28	Dijon-Style Deviled Eggs	Turkey and Artichokes	Gingery Sea Bass

8.   Conclusion

Food is medicine. We know this on a subconscious level. We know that eating right and eating healthy will contribute to our living healthier and happier lives. But somehow, we find it more and more difficult to eat healthy foods as we grow older.

This isn't entirely our fault. The availability and cultural popularity of processed foods make it all too easy to consume entire "meals" that are almost devoid of beneficial nutrients. Worse, when we do consume whole foods, we're far more likely to consume them in the form of animal products than we are of plant products.

You, however, came to this book for a reason. On some level, you know that the typical western diet is harmful to your body and your health. Whether you're struggling with a chronic illness yourself, watching someone else struggle with chronic health conditions, or simply looking to learn the truth about the foods you put into your body, you now have all the knowledge you need to create meals for yourself that are rich in all the essential actual nutrients your body needs to survive.

After having read this book, you now understand the role nutrients play in the body when they enter the digestive system. You understand how your gut is connected to the other systems in your body. Most importantly, you understand how the immune system works, and how the nutrients that we consume through food play a key role in our immune health. A nutrient-poor diet will eventually lead to poor immune function, which makes us vulnerable to infections, auto-immune conditions, and cancer growths.

The 11 "superfoods" listed in this book are just a starting point. The key to a healthy diet, ultimately, is variety. The more different kinds of plant-based foods you can introduce into your diet, the happier your gut and body will be. Any meal that's based on whole plant foods is one that you can be sure is rich in a number of beneficial nutrients, all of which will promote the health of your gut, your immune system, and the other organs of your body.

The kindest thing you can do for yourself is to avoid processed foods as much as possible. If you've learned nothing else from this book, it's that the closer your food gets to the form it took when it came out of the ground, the better. While I advocate primarily for a plant-based diet in this book, limited quantities of meat and animal products are far from harmful when consumed in the context of plant- based, nutrient-dense meals.

The number one actually takeaway from this book is this: the less natural your food is when you buy it, the lower its nutritional value. And the lower the nutritional value of your meals, the more vulnerable you are to health conditions of all kinds.

No longer do you have to struggle with painful auto-immune conditions or live dependent on a toxic cocktail of medications. Almost all of the diseases that plague us in the 21st century can be traced back to nutrient-poor diets, and almost all of those diseases can be both prevented and treated with diets that are nutrient-rich. No longer does "eating healthy" have to be a painful, difficult regime, in which you are not "allowed" to indulge in the foods that you enjoy most.

Rather, start your transition to healthy living by simply adding more of these eleven superfoods to your meals. Find opportunities to swap out pasta and meats for quinoa, potatoes, and beans. Add nuts and leafy greens to your meals whenever possible. Take advantage of the wide variety of recipes available on the internet that contain all of these superfoods and more. Most importantly, have fun. Enjoy the new strength and vitality that you experience as your body begins to eat the way that it was meant to eat, and function the way that it was meant to function.

9.   Index

Printed in Great Britain
by Amazon

11132717R00068